Qualifying as a Nonprofit Tax-Exempt Organization

QUALIFYING AS A NONPROFIT TAX-EXEMPT ORGANIZATION

A Guide for Attorneys, Accountants, and Executive Management

ROBERT N. SUGHRUE and
MICHELLE L. KOPNSKI

QUORUM BOOKS
New York • Westport, Connecticut • London

Library of Congress Cataloging-in-Publication Data

Sughrue, Robert N.
Qualifying as a nonprofit tax-exempt organization : a guide for attorneys, accountants, and executive management / Robert N. Sughrue and Michelle L. Kopnski.
p. cm.
Includes bibliographical references and index.
ISBN 0-89930-483-4 (alk. paper)
1. Corporations, Nonprofit—Taxation—United States.
2. Charitable uses, trusts, and foundations—Taxation—United States. I. Kopnski, Michelle L. II. Title.
KF6449.S84 1991
343.7306'68—dc20
[347.303668] 90-42965

British Library Cataloguing in Publication Data is available.

Library of Congress Catalog Card Number: 90-42965
ISBN: 0-89930-483-4

First published in 1991

Quorum Books, 88 Post Road West, Westport, CT 06881
An imprint of Greenwood Publishing Group, Inc.

Printed in the United States of America

The paper used in this book complies with the Permanent Paper Standard issued by the National Information Standards Organization (Z39.48-1984).

10 9 8 7 6 5 4 3 2 1

Contents

Acknowledgments

This publication would not have been possible without the efforts of five individual contributors. The authors express their sincere gratitude to John J. Kopnski, Louise S. Kopnski, John C. Raley, Barbara L. Kachurik, and Beverly K. Sughrue.

John and Louise Kopnski were responsible for proofreading and editing the legal sections of this text and provided constant support. Their dedicated efforts enhanced the integrity of the work and relieved the authors of a substantial burden.

John Raley contributed numerous hours proofreading the entire text and providing relevant editorial comments with respect to the contents of this work. His insight was an invaluable aid in bringing this project to a timely conclusion.

Barbara Kachurik's support in the preliminary proofreading and editing process proved to be a valuable time-saver as the book progressed toward completion.

Beverly Sughrue was responsible for typing the initial draft of this work as well as coordinating numerous rewrites, corrections, and amplifications. Throughout this arduous process, she demonstrated professionalism at its highest level.

Qualifying as a Nonprofit Tax-Exempt Organization

1

Exempt Organizations: An Overview

INTRODUCTION

Any analysis of complex subject matter requires the analyst to have, at a minimum, a general understanding of the basic terminology relating to that subject. More important, the analyst must be cognizant of the framework and environment impacting the dynamics of the subject to be analyzed. The authors feel that it is particularly important for students of exempt organizations to become thoroughly familiar with certain terms that will be used throughout this book, and to gain an appreciation of the social, legal, and political environment in which tax-exempt organizations operate. It must, therefore, be understood that the objectives of this chapter are twofold:

- To identify, for the reader, a number of terms that will appear in this and future chapters and to qualify the meaning of these terms within the scope of this book;
- To identify environmental factors that influence exempt organizations with respect to their business decisions and modus operandi.

WHAT IS AN EXEMPT ORGANIZATION?

Within the context of this book, the term "exempt organization" means any organization described in the Internal Revenue Code as not being required to pay federal income tax on earnings realized through routine operations. A discussion of individual state statutes and the peculiarities among states will not be pursued.

It must be pointed out that exemption from federal income tax does not necessarily preclude the imposition of other federal taxes. Tax-exempt organizations may, at some time in the term of their existence, be subject to federal excise taxes. In addition, with few exceptions, exempt organizations are subject to federal unemployment taxes and employers' social security tax. Other taxes such as unrelated business income tax that can be imposed on exempt organizations are discussed throughout this book.

THE NONPROFIT ORGANIZATION VERSUS THE TAX-EXEMPT ORGANIZATION

Contrary to popular belief, the term "nonprofit organization," or as some prefer, "not-for-profit organization," is not synonymous with the term "exempt organization." Put simply, the latter term relates exclusively to organizations that are not subject to federal income tax as discussed within the preceding paragraph. The nonprofit organization may or may not be exempt from federal income tax. The term "nonprofit" implies that earnings (revenues in excess of expenses) are retained in the organization to further the organization's purpose rather than being distributed to investors and/or other entities that contributed capital for motives of obtaining a return on investment. Both nonprofit and exempt organizations fully expect to realize revenues in excess of expense (profit). This expectation is rather obvious. Continuous losses will necessarily lead to insolvency and thereby paralyze the organization with respect to its continuance as a going concern. Some nonprofit organizations pay taxes on their profits, whereas all exempt organizations do not, unless the exempt organization is subject to unrelated business income tax (see Chapter 4). The distinction between nonprofit and exempt can be summarized by the following axiom: all exempt organizations are nonprofit; however, nonprofit organizations are not all exempt organizations.

GENERAL CHARACTERISTICS OF AN EXEMPT ORGANIZATION

Tax-exempt organizations are generally nonprofit organizations formed with a mission designed to serve the public interest in a manner that provides benefits to society as a whole. Examples of exempt organizations include churches, universities, crop cooperatives, health-care research organizations, health education organizations, educational television stations, philanthropic private foundations, and so on. The number of exempt organizational types appears almost limitless. Most exempt organizations are described within Internal Revenue Code Section 501(c). This section has twenty-five subdivisions (501(c)(1) through 501(c)(25)). These subdivisions describe general exempt organizational types and the related qualifying factors. For example, Code Section 501(c)(5) exempts (from federal income tax) labor, agricultural, or horticultural organizations. As the astute reader can imagine, the term labor organizations, in the generic sense, encompasses several types of organizations—teacher unions and professional organizations, auto workers, steamfitters, transportation workers, steel workers, and so on. Similarly, there are several subsets of agricultural and horticultural organizations. Chapter 3 provides an in-depth analysis of each subdivision of Code Section 501(c). There are a few other code sections that describe other types of exempt organizations. These organizations are also discussed in Chapter 3.

Exempt organizations do not necessarily have to be incorporated. Tax exemption can be recognized for clubs, associations, cooperatives, and trusts.

The functions of exempt organizations can vary widely. The authors prefer to classify exempt organizations by function in three general categories: service organizations, sales organizations, and hybrid organizations. By the authors' definition, exempt service organizations are those that rely exclusively on contributions and/or membership assessments for their support (revenue). Examples include churches, community chest funds, and business leagues. Sales organizations rely exclusively on external funds derived from the sale of a product or service emanating from the performance of the organization's exempt function. Examples include some research organizations and exempt credit unions. It should be noted, however, that the organizations that only carry on a trade or business (as defined within the Internal Revenue Code) are generally not recognized as exempt. The third classification of exempt organizations, the hybrid type, is probably the largest and most diverse category. These organizations are generally supported by a combination of grants/contributions and funds derived from the performance of their exempt function. Consider, for instance, an amateur sports organization. In all likelihood, revenues are derived from private contributions as well as ticket sales. Another example of a hybrid organization might be an animal welfare organization.

ITEMS TO CONSIDER WHEN CONTEMPLATING THE FORMATION OF AN EXEMPT ORGANIZATION

In determining whether or not a contemplated organization qualifies for exempt recognition, the founders must consider myriad facts and circumstances related to the proposed organization's mission, structure, core activities, and limitations related thereto, staffing needs, physical locations, posture on lobbying effort, sources of support, and a number of other factors. Similarly, existing organizations desiring to obtain exempt recognition and/or reorganize for purposes of maintaining their existing exemption must make several specific determinations relating to their structure, activity, purpose, and, in some cases, changes in structure, activity, and purpose. These determinations are critical. In the final analysis, these factors govern which Internal Revenue Code Section applies to the organization. The governing code section is of utmost importance in that restrictions on an organization's permitted activities are more stringent under certain code sections than they are under other sections. For instance, organizations recognized as exempt pursuant to Code Section 501(c)(3) are prohibited from engaging in substantial lobbying efforts, whereas Code Section 501(c)(4) organizations are not subject to these restrictions.

The process of organizing an exempt organization or reorganizing an existing organization with respect to maintaining or obtaining exempt recognition is a complex process. Critical determinations cannot be made unilaterally—a joint effort is required. Operational, legal, and financial personnel must draw on their respective areas of expertise to ensure the successful achievement of the desired end.

OTHER CODE SECTIONS

The issues related to tax-exemption are not isolated. There are direct Internal Revenue Code sections which define the various types of exempt organizations. The primary example is Code Section 501. Other indirect code sections impose various requirements and restrictions on exempt recognition. Exhibit 1-1 lists a number of code sections applicable to exempt organizations.

In addition to the sections referenced in Exhibit 1-1 there are several other sections applicable to exempt organizations. These sections relate to tax-exempt trusts and excise taxes imposed upon private foundations. Chapter 3 will discuss tax-exempt trusts in depth. Similarly, Chapters 2 and 5 discuss the 501(c)(3) organization and the differentiation between public charities and private foundations.

Exhibit 1-1
Exempt Organizations—Applicable Code Sections

Internal Revenue Code References	Subjects Addressed
Section 502-Feeder Organizations	Addresses organizations having a primary purpose of carrying on a trade or a business that normally would not be exempt under Section 501 but are exempt because all of the profits are payable to an organization recognized as exempt under Section 501.
Section 503-Requirements for Exemption	Denies exemption to certain organizations that engage in a specified prohibited transaction.
Section 504-After an Organization Ceases to Qualify for Exemption Under Section 501(c)(3) Because of Substantial Lobbying.	Prevents a 501(c)(3) which has lost its exemption because of substantial lobbying from being recognized as exempt under Section 501(c)(4).
Section 505-Requirement for 501(c)(9), 501(c)(17), and 501(c)20 Organizations	Describes additional nondiscrimination requirements for exempt entities organized for the purpose of providing certain benefits (insurance, pension, etc.)
Section 507-Termination of Private Foundation Status	Defines the method(s) and circumstances which a 501(c)(3) private foundation can terminate the private foundation status.
Section 508-Special Rules with Respect to Section 501(c)(3) Organizations	Limits instances where organizations can seek exempt recognition pursuant to Section 501(c)(3); imposes notification requirements with respect to both exempt recognition and avoidance of private foundation status; imposes requirements with respect to the organization's governing instruments.
Section 509-Private Foundation Defined	Defines, by exception, private foundations, i.e., what 501(c)(3) organizations can be excluded from private foundation status because of their respective levels of public support. Defines the term "gross investment income" for purposes of computing taxes imposed pursuant to Section 511.

Exhibit 1-1 (continued)

Internal Revenue Code References	Subjects Addressed
Section 511-Imposition of Tax on Unrelated Business Income of Charitable., Etc., Organizations	Imposes the regular corporate tax on the unrelated business income of exempt organizations unless the exempt organization is a trust.
Section 512-Unrelated Business Taxable Income	Defines the term unrelated business income for purposes of the imposition of tax addressed within Section 511.
Section 513-Unrelated Trade or Business	Defines the term unrelated trade or business for purposes of determining the presence of qualifying conditions references within Section 512.
Section 514-Unrelated Debt Financed Income	Defines unrelated debt financed income and deductions for purposes of arriving at the appropriate level of unrelated business taxable income addressed within Section 512.
Section 515-Taxes of Foreign Countries and Possessions of the United States	In certain circumstances, permits organizations subject to taxes imposed pursuant to Section 511 to offset these taxes by taxes of foreign countries and possessions of the United States.
Section 521-Exemption of Farmers' Cooperatives From Tax	Exempts certain farmers' cooperatives from taxation when such cooperatives are formed for purposes of realizing the benefits of joint selling and purchasing.
Section 527-Political Organizations	Exempts defined political organizations from most taxes. Defines taxable income for these organizations.
Section 528-Certain Homeowner Associations	Exempts defined homeowner associations from most taxes. Defines taxable income for these organizations.
Section 1443-Foreign Tax-Exempt Organizations	Subjects foreign tax-exempt organizations to withholding on unrelated business taxable income and gross investment income.

INTERNAL REVENUE CODE, REGULATIONS, PROCEDURES, AND OTHER REFERENCES

Thus far, the discussions contained within this chapter relate exclusively to Internal Revenue Code references. It is imperative to note that reliance on the code is generally insufficient with respect to reaching substantive conclusions and/or decisions regarding matters related to exempt organizations. Due to the complexity of the subject, one must become familiar with the basic reference sources emanating directly from the Internal Revenue Code. Accordingly, the following discussions are intended to provide such a guide.

First, it must be understood that the Internal Revenue Code is comprised of a series of U.S. tax laws. As previously stated, it cannot be relied on as a sole source reference in the decision-making process. The code is supported by regulations. Regulations are the Treasury Department's official interpretation of the Internal Revenue Code. The regulations contain clarifications and explanations of the various code sections with respect to complying with the requirements imposed by the code.

Revenue rulings differ from regulations. Rulings represent the Internal Revenue Service's (henceforth IRS) interpretation of the code relating to the facts and circumstances related to a specific situation.

In addition to regulations and rulings, there are several other sources of reference available to management staffs of tax-exempt organizations. For instance, matters relating to procedural compliance with respect to provisions of the code are referenced in formal Revenue Procedures. Revenue Procedures are formal statements of the IRS relating to procedural matters such as an appeals process, advance rulings, and/or other determinations.

In certain situations, the IRS will issue unpublished rulings, sometimes referred to as letter rulings. These differ somewhat for the Revenue Rulings and Revenue Procedures. Rulings and procedures generally relate to all taxpayers; they are formal, published statements of how the tax law is to be applied and what taxpayers have to do to comply with the tax law. The key word here is *published.* Revenue rulings and procedures are published nationally and can be relied on by *all* taxpayers in circumstances similar to the circumstance addressed within the respective rulings and procedures. By contrast, unpublished rulings apply *only* to a specific set of circumstances. Because of this, their usefulness in terms of the decision-making process within exempt organizations is limited. Nevertheless, they do sometimes serve as a good informational source. A taxpayer can request an unpublished ruling from either the National Office of the IRS (a private letter ruling) or from a district office (a determination letter). Private letter rulings can be revoked or changed but such occurrences (revocations or modifications) are rare. Generally, a taxpayer can comfortably rely on the substance of a private letter ruling. Determination letters can be revoked much more easily.

For instance, a district director, upon examination of a taxpayer's return, can unilaterally revoke a determination letter. In some situations, specifically those where a district director cannot make a determination, the district director may request advice from the National Office. In these situations, the National Office will issue a technical advice memorandum.

In addition to relying on the aforementioned documents for purposes of making decisions in a tax-exempt environment, managers should be aware of the various technical publications available as a reference source. Two of the better-known publishers in this area are Commerce Clearing House Incorporated and Prentice-Hall Incorporated.

FINANCIAL CONSIDERATIONS

Managers in tax-exempt environments cannot ignore financial issues just because of the nonprofit status of their respective organizations. While pure tax issues are critically important to the exempt entity, the absence of adequate financial planning can result in insolvency and thereby dilute and/or render worthless even the best decisions with respect to matters of taxation. Notwithstanding the preceding statement, readers should be cautioned that taxation issues are not necessarily mutually exclusive from financial issues.

The lack of mutual exclusivity is demonstrated in a number of ways. Decisions emanating from a tax perspective can have a profound impact on financial systems. For instance, a decision to terminate a 501(c)(3) organization's private foundation status can, and probably will, require the organization to expand its accounting system. Each cash receipt must be analyzed by type to determine whether or not the prospective five-year support tests are met. In this example, the accounting system must be capable of identifying and grouping grants and contributions from (a) government sources, (b) public sources, and (c) private sources. The accounting system must also be capable of differentiating between grants, contributions, and income recognized in connection with the performance of exempt activities. In situations such as these, accounting managers must gain a thorough understanding of the appropriate tax laws so that management has a quick and efficient way to monitor compliance.

The primary financial consideration in a tax-exempt organization involves its system of internal controls. This control environment should be such that it provides reasonable assurance that errors and omissions (whether deliberate or not) are prevented or, if not prevented, detected on a timely basis. A poor system of internal controls can result in incorrect recording of transactions and may lead to incorrect decisions with respect to matters involving taxation. For example, an accounting clerk who is not familiar with the reporting requirements related to unrelated business taxable income may record this income as a public grant or contribution. If the misclassification is not detected, the organization would probably fail to report properly and be subject to penalty and interest charges.

The situation described in the preceding example could have been prevented had the proper control environment been provided. In this instance, the presence of an accounting manual explaining what unrelated business taxable income is and how to record it would have prevented the problem from occurring (assuming of course that the accounting clerk read the manual). Supervisory review, a detective control, would at least have detected the problem in time to avoid penalty and interest charges.

Chapter 7 discusses, in depth, the necessity and importance of internal controls within an exempt organization.

EXEMPT ORGANIZATIONS—THE CURRENT ENVIRONMENT

Exempt organizations do not enjoy the sociopolitical status they once enjoyed. The proliferation of exempt organizations as well as the expansion and diversification of established exempt organizations have made the business community, the general public, and regulatory authorities more aware of exempt organizations' functions and business philosophies. In some cases exempt organizations have been the object of public criticism and have found themselves under the watchful eyes of both the IRS, Congress, and state/municipal taxing authorities.

The largest issue relating to exempt organizations involves a general complaint that exempt organizations have an unfair market advantage over their taxable counterparts because federal income and other taxes do not have to be recovered in an exempt organization's pricing structure. There is some validity to this criticism. In response to public scrutiny, exempt organizations have examined themselves and have responded in a number of different ways.

One of the most common responses has been to reorganize the core structure of the organization. There are several benefits to this approach. In a typical reorganization, a holding company may be formed. The formation of the holding company results in a structure which isolates tax-exempt and taxable functions. Certain activities that were once performed in the original exempt organization can then be assigned to other organizations reporting to the holding company. This action purifies the original exempt organization in that activities that may not be considered exempt are effectively removed and placed in taxable entities. Although the taxable entities are subject to federal income tax, taxes would probably also be incurred by the original exempt entity in the form of unrelated business income tax. Since, in the short run, there is no overall tax advantage, one might question the necessity of the reorganization. The major benefit is that the holding company can freely expand into areas which the former organization could not without jeopardizing its exemption. Reorganizations of this nature were once popular within the banking industry, albeit tax exemption was not the driving force. In recent years exempt organizations (particularly health-care providers) have adopted this practice on a wide-scale basis.

As illustrated in the preceding paragraph, exempt organizations are frequently expanding and diversifying. The management staffs of these organizations must be cognizant of the tax impact of expansion and/or diversification. Exhibit 1-2 contains some of the questions managers must consider when contemplating a change in structure, operations, or both.

There are obviously many more questions to resolve; however, the short list appearing in Exhibit 1-2 illustrates the line of reasoning managers must follow when making decisions concerning the future of their organization.

Exhibit 1-2
Organizational Questions for Managers

1. Are the contemplated operations consistent with one or more of the "exempt purposes" contained within the existing governing instruments?

2. Do the contemplated operations fall within any internal revenue code exemption category?

3. Will the contemplated operations require a substantial lobbying effort on a continuous basis?

Exhibit 1-2 (continued)

4. What sources of support will the operation attract?
5. What type of initial funding will be required?
6. Will the activities of the contemplated operation consist solely of operating a trade or business? If no, to what extent?
7. Will assets have to be transferred?
8. Will the contemplated operation be part of the exempt entity (operating division) or will a separate corporation be formed?

ANNUAL FILING REQUIREMENTS FOR EXEMPT ORGANIZATIONS

In all but a few instances, exempt organizations must file an annual tax return. In most cases, exempt organizations can satisfy the annual filing requirement by filing Form 990—Return of an Organization Exempt from Income Tax. An organization's completed Form 990 must be made available for public inspection. For 1988, the IRS estimated the average time necessary to complete Form 990 as follows:

Recording Keeping	90 Hours, 53 Minutes
Learning about the Law or the Form	8 Hours, 04 Minutes
Preparing the Form	12 Hours, 41 Minutes
Copying, Assembling, and Sending the Form to the IRS	48 Minutes

The above data translates into 112½ hours per year which equates to 70 percent of a full-time equivalent employee for one month. There are certain organizations that do not have to file Form 990. Organizations exempt from tax under Section 501(a) (churches, interchurch organizations, a below-college-level school affiliated with a church, religious orders, instrumentalities of the United States, etc.) do not have to file Form 990. If an organization's gross receipts are $25,000 or less, an annual Form 990 need not be filed. However, the IRS strongly encourages such organizations to file anyway.

An organization which is exempt from federal tax under Section 501(c)(3) and which is a private foundation is not required to file Form 990. However, it must file Form 990-PF—Return of Private Foundation. This form must also be filed by certain nonexempt trusts. Form 990-PF is much longer and more complicated than Form 990 because of certain restrictions and requirements exclusive to private foundations. As was the case with Form 990, Form 990-PF must be made available for public inspection. For 1988, the IRS estimated the average time necessary to complete Form 990-PF as follows:

Record Keeping	130 Hours, 06 Minutes
Learning about the Law or the Form	21 Hours, 25 Minutes
Preparing the Form	25 Hours, 25 Minutes
Copying, Assembling, and Sending the Form to the IRS	16 Minutes

The above data translates into approximately 177.2 hours per year, which equates to a little over one full month of an employee's time.

Organizations exempt under Code Section 501(c)(21) (Black Lung Benefit Trusts) are not required to file a Form 990. However, these organizations must file Form 990-BL—Information and Initial Excise Tax Return for Black Lung Benefit Trusts and Certain Related Persons. When compared to Forms 990 and 990-PF, this form is relatively simple to complete. The IRS estimates that the form and the supporting schedules can be completed in approximately 4½ hours. The completed form must be made available for public inspection.

Organizations exempt under Code Section 521(a) are not required to file Form 990. These organizations must file Form 990-C—Farmers' Cooperative Association Income Tax Return. This form closely resembles a tax return of a nonexempt corporation because revenues in excess of expenses are taxable at regular corporate rates. This form is rather lengthy. The IRS estimated average completion time is as follows:

Record Keeping	69 Hours, 07 Minutes
Learning about the Law or the Form	17 Hours, 49 Minutes
Preparing the Form	34 Hours, 37 Minutes
Copying, Assembling, and Sending the Form to the IRS	4 Hours, 17 Minutes

In terms of full-time equivalence, Form 990-C will take 80 percent of a man-month.

Political organizations exempt under Code Section 527 must file Form 1120-POL—Income Tax Return for Certain Political Organizations, rather than Form 990. Form 1120-POL resembles a regular corporate income tax form because earnings derived from investing unused contributions are subject to tax. The tax rate is the highest corporate rate then in effect. The IRS estimated completion time is:

Record Keeping	14 Hours, 07 Minutes
Learning about the Law or the Form	6 Hours, 23 Minutes
Preparing the Form	15 Hours, 17 Minutes
Copying, Assembling, and Sending the Form to the IRS	2 Hours, 25 Minutes

In other words, it will take approximately 37 hours or one full week of an employee's time to complete Form 1120-POL.

Organizations exempt under Code Section 528, Certain Homeowners Associations, must file Form 1120-H instead of Form 990. Like political organizations, homeowners associations have a potential tax liability. Income components such as interest, nonmember usage fees, and so on, are subject to tax (flat 30% rate for 1988). Because of the potential tax liability, Form 1120-H resembles a regular corporate tax form. The IRS estimated average completion time is:

Record Keeping	9 Hours, 20 Minutes
Learning about the Law or the Form	4 Hours, 12 Minutes
Preparing the Form	10 Hours, 12 Minutes
Copying, Assembling, and Sending the Form to the IRS	1 Hour, 30 Minutes

Form 1120-H takes the equivalent of 20 percent of a man-month.

The above discussions relate only to annual filing requirements pursuant to an organization's exempt status. Each of the forms has several supporting schedules associated with it. For instance, a typical Form 990 requires supporting schedules showing, at a minimum, the detail of investments, fixed assets, deferred charges, and loans to officers.

In addition to the annual filing requirements, exempt organizations must file quarterly wage and salary statements (generally Form 941), and they must deposit payroll related tax withholdings within the prescribed time limits.

Organizations that file Form 990 may be required to file another return (in addition to Form 990). If organizations have unrelated business taxable income, they are required to file Form 990-T—Exempt Organization Business Income Tax Return. This form resembles a corporate tax return and is used to compute the organization's yearly tax liability. Unrelated business income tax is discussed in Chapter 4.

SUMMARY

The subject matter related to tax-exempt organizations is complex. The subject of tax exemption cannot be reviewed in a vacuum; a substantial portion of the Internal Revenue Code devotes itself to the cans and cannots of tax-exempt entities. Managers and administrators of tax-exempt entities must be cognizant of the various tax intricacies related to their respective organizations. In this regard, there are many published references available to assist in the decision-making process. The IRS code is merely a starting point. There are underlying regulations, published procedures, and other less formal rulings and determinations that must be reviewed in their appropriate context.

Tax-exempt organizations are similar to taxable organizations with respect to their mutual need to maintain financial liquidity. The term "tax-exempt" does not necessarily mean that an organization cannot realize a profit from its operations. The distinction lies within the fact that tax-exempt entities necessarily retain profits to continue performing their exempt functions. Profits realized by tax-exempt entities are not available for distribution to shareholders and/or other investors expecting a return on investment.

In all but a few instances, tax-exempt organizations must file annual tax returns. In addition, tax-exempt organizations are generally subject to the same withholding requirements imposed upon taxable entities; employer-paid payroll taxes are also imposed upon tax-exempt organizations.

Administrators and financial managers must keep themselves abreast of the various regulations applicable to their respective organizations, regardless of the basis of tax exemption. Tax matters require a substantial amount of management oversight and staff time. Familiarity with the underlying tax requirements is an essential element in the successful management of a tax-exempt organization.

2

The 501(c)(3) Tax-Exempt Organization

The Section 501(c)(3) charitable organization is by far the broadest type of tax-exempt organization. This status is desired because contributions made to such charitable organizations are tax deductible by the donor, whereas contributions to organizations falling under other tax-exempt classifications are not.[1] According to the Internal Revenue Code Section 501(c)(3), an organization (corporation, community chest fund, foundation, or trust) seeking to obtain tax-exempt status under that classification must be organized and operated exclusively for at least one of the stated exempt purposes. Such purposes are religious, charitable, scientific, testing for public safety, literary, educational, fostering national or international amateur sports competition (but only if no part of its activities involves the provision of athletic facilities or equipment), and preventing cruelty to children or animals. In addition, no part of the net earnings of the organization may inure to the benefit of any private shareholder or individual. No substantial part of the activities of the organization may consist of carrying on propaganda, or otherwise attempting to influence legislation; and finally, the organization may not participate in, or intervene in, any political campaign on behalf of or in opposition to any candidate for public office. The remainder of this chapter will be devoted to the analysis of each specific requirement which must be met by a charitable organization in order to qualify for tax-exempt status under Section 501(c)(3).

The first requirement for qualification under Section 501(c)(3) is that the organization be organized and operated exclusively for one of the exempt purposes listed therein. The regulations separate this requirement into two distinct tests: the "organizational test" and the "operational test." It is of utmost importance to recognize that both tests must be independently satisfied. An organization that fails to satisfy the organizational test will not qualify for tax-exempt status; and one that has qualified but does not conduct its operations in compliance with the operational test will lose its tax-exempt status.

ORGANIZATIONAL TEST

The organizational test has been in effect since 26 July 1959. Any organization determined to be tax-exempt prior to that date did not have its exemption revoked for failure to meet the new organizational test. However, any organization seeking a new determination of exemption subsequent to that date must have a governing instrument that specifically limits the organization's purposes and powers in accordance with the organizational test.[2]

In order to satisfy the organizational test, the governing instrument of the organization must specifically limit the purpose of such organization to one or more of the exempt purposes set out in Section 501(c)(3). Additionally, its governing instrument must not expressly empower the organization to engage, other than as an insubstantial part of its activities, in activities which in themselves are not in furtherance of one or more exempt purpose.[3] A governing instrument can be a corporate charter (articles of incorporation), articles of association, a trust indenture, or any other written instrument by which an organization is created.[4]

The organizational test itself, then, has two distinct parts: (1) the organization's statement of its purpose or purposes, and (2) the organization's statement of its powers.

The organization's stated purposes should fall within the boundaries of those enumerated in Section 501(c)(3).[5] Stated purposes beyond those boundaries cause the organization to fail the organizational test. It is acceptable in many instances to restate the language of Section 501(c)(3) in the governing instrument, or at least to limit the stated purposes by reference to Section 501(c)(3). For example, a governing instrument which states that the organization is formed for "charitable purposes'' is sufficient for purposes of the organizational test.[6] A governing instrument which limits the organization to ''scientific and educational'' purposes is also sufficient for purposes of the organizational test.

One caution here is that terms used in the governing instrument are given their ''generally accepted meaning.'' However, the law of the state in which the organization is created controls how the meaning of the terms is construed. Therefore, if an organization contends that the terms have a different meaning under state law than their generally accepted meaning, the organization must establish such meaning by clear and convincing reference to relevant court decisions, opinions of the state attorney general, or other applicable state law.[7] For example, an organization whose purposes are stated in its governing instrument as ''charitable and philanthropic'' would not meet the organizational test. This is because ''philanthropic'' has no generally accepted meaning, and therefore, the activities permitted may be beyond the boundaries of Section 501(c)(3) purposes. However, if the organization contends that, under the laws of the state in which the organization is created, the term ''philanthropic,'' by definition, falls within the boundaries of Section 501(c)(3) purposes, the burden is on the organization to establish such meaning by clear and convincing evidence.[8]

The statement of the organization's powers is also determinative in concluding that an organization has met the organizational test. An organization must be certain that its governing instrument does not expressly empower it to engage in activities, other than as an insubstantial part of its activities, which are not in furtherance of its exempt purpose.[9] This means that even if an organization's purpose or purposes fall within the boundaries of Section 501(c)(3), the mere power to engage in substantial activity not in furtherance of those purposes would cause the organization to fail the organizational test. This is true regardless of whether the organization ever actually exercises such powers. For example, an organization organized for charitable purposes within the meaning of Section 501(c)(3) would not meet the organizational test if it was also empowered to operate a retail store or to engage in a manufacturing business. Prudence would suggest that the governing instrument should, in some manner, indicate that the organization is not empowered to conduct any activities which would extend beyond the boundaries of Section 501(c)(3).

The Treasury Regulations are most decisive with regard to the authorization of legislative or political powers for a Section 501(c)(3) organization. The Regulations state that an organization will not meet the organizational test if its governing instrument expressly empowers it to devote more than an insubstantial part of its activities to attempting to influence legislation by propaganda or otherwise; or, to directly or indirectly participate in or intervene in (including the publication or distribution of statements) any political campaign on behalf of or in opposition to any candidate for public office; or, to have objectives and to engage in activities which characterize it as an ''action'' organization as defined in the Regulations. (''Action'' organizations will be discussed later in this chapter.)[10]

A final mandate of the organizational test is that the assets of the organization must be permanently dedicated to an exempt purpose.[11] This can be assured either by a specific provision in the organization's governing instrument or by operation of the law of the state in which the organization is formed so that, upon dissolution of the organization, the organization's assets would be distributed for one or more exempt purposes; or would be distributed to the Federal, state, or local government for a public purpose; or would be distributed by a court to another organization to be used according to the judgment of the court to accomplish as nearly as possible the general purposes of the dissolved organization.[12] Notice here that a specific provision in the governing instrument may not be required if the law of the state in which the organization is formed provides for an acceptable distribution of assets. However, as was noted previously in this chapter, when an organization intends to rely upon state law to interpret, supplement, or give meaning to its governing instrument, it is incumbent upon the organization to prove the meaning of the state law to the IRS by clear and convincing evidence.[13]

An organization should very carefully examine state law before making the decision to rely upon it in lieu of placing a specific provision in its governing instrument. It seems most prudent, regardless of state law, to simply include a specific provision regarding asset distribution. This would alleviate the need to research and brief state law extensively, and would also protect the organization's exemption should state law ever change.

In summary, the organizational test can be thought of as simply a matter of form whereby the IRS will examine the organization's governing instrument to determine if the proper language has been included and whether the powers granted to the organization fall within the boundaries of Section 501(c)(3). Additionally, the IRS will look for language which permanently dedicates the assets of the organization to an exempt purpose. Because the organizational test is so easily satisfied, the most effective approach in applying for tax-exempt status is to include the appropriate language and powers in the governing instrument. There is some authority to suggest that the organizational test may be met by factors beyond the governing instrument, such as bylaw provisions limiting the purposes and powers of the organization or an examination of the circumstances surrounding the actual operations of the organization. For example, the tax court granted tax-exempt status to a chiropractic society whose bylaws, but not its articles of incorporation, restricted it to only exempt purposes and activities. The court stated that the determination of tax-exempt status should not be based solely upon an examination of the organization's stated purposes in its governing instrument; rather, the court held that such determination must be made only after review of all of the surrounding facts and circumstances.[14]

Case holdings such as this can create misguided security for any organization that hopes to satisfy the organizational test without including the appropriate language in its governing instrument. It should be particularly noted that if an organization intends to rely on anything other than appropriate language in its governing instrument to show compliance with the organizational test, the burden is placed directly on the organization to produce sufficient evidence as proof of such compliance. This route, in the vast majority of cases, will certainly be more burdensome and risky than would be drafting the appropriate governing instrument or amending the existing governing instrument to meet the traditional requirements of the organizational test.

OPERATIONAL TEST

In contrast to the organizational test which may be satisfied fairly routinely by a detailed tracing of the language set forth by the code and regulations, the operational test delves directly into an examination of the workings and actual activities of the would-be Section 501(c)(3) organization. An organization will be regarded as "operated exclusively" for one or more exempt purpose only if it:

- Engages primarily in activities which accomplish one or more exempt purposes as listed in Section 501(c)(3);
- No part of its net earnings inure to the benefit of private shareholders or individuals; and
- It is not classified as an "action" organization.[15]

According to the regulations, an organization will not be regarded as operated exclusively for exempt purposes if more than an insubstantial part of its activities is not in furtherance of an exempt purpose.[16] The regulations, then, do not completely prohibit nonexempt activities such as the operation of a nonrelated trade or business. However, an organization will not meet the operational test if the nonexempt activity constitutes more than an insubstantial part of the total activities of the organization. This really means that an organization must be operated "primarily" for a tax-exempt purpose.

Unfortunately, no legislation or regulations have ever been promulgated which clearly define an "insubstantial part" of an organization's activities or set forth rules as to the point at which the level of business activities would threaten the organization's exempt status. An organization is left to examine the facts and circumstances of its own activities and to continuously monitor its activities to make certain that most of its activities are in furtherance of its exempt purpose.

An organization should begin its analysis of its activies by examining each activity in terms of whether such activity could be categorized as a purely exempt activity; that is, clearly related to the organization's tax-exempt purpose. Other activities which are more clearly business ventures must be closely analyzed to determine if they jeopardize the organization's tax-exempt status by rising to the level of "substantial."

Several factors are considered by the IRS and by the courts in determining whether the business activities have exceeded permissible limits. These factors set up a sort of "balancing test" by which to make an overall judgment. The factors include the actual proportion of the exempt and business activities to total activities, the commercial viability of the activity, the existence of and amount of profits from the activity, whether any actual profits are used for exempt activities, and whether the profits inure in any manner to the organization's shareholders or to private individuals.[17]

Obviously, as an overall limit, an organization should strive to keep the total amount of nonexempt (business) activity as only an incidental part of its overall operations. This means that the proportion of exempt activities to total activities should be much larger than the proportion of business activities to total activities. This analysis examines the business activities relative to the exempt activities rather than analyzing them on an individual basis. Clearly, it is better to have a greater proportion of exempt activities in relation to the proportion of business activities. This is perhaps the most significant factor in judging how "exclusively" the organization is operated for exempt purposes.

Commercial viability has become an increasingly important concern. It deals with the ability of any business activity to compete with taxable business competitors. This factor examines the character of the activity and, to a great extent, its ability to make a profit. Commercial viability, in this sense, does not concern itself with whether a profit was actually made; it is sufficient if it is possible to make a profit from the activity. For example, in *Scripture Press Foundation v. U.S.*,[18] a religious organization's sale of instructional religious literature (arguably a religious activity), was found to be carried on in a manner that gave the activity a commercial character because sales were made in such a manner that a profit could have been realized. Similarly, in *Federation Pharmacy Services, Inc. v. Commissioner*,[19] tax exempt status was denied to a pharmacy that sold drugs at cost to the elderly and the handicapped. Again, the commercial character of the operations, not the lack of profits, was determinative of whether the pharmacy was operated for an exempt purpose.

While it is clear that commercial viability can override the lack of profits in determining that an organization is not operated exclusively for an exempt purpose, the lack of profits, or the existence of only a limited amount of profits would probably be considered by the IRS or a court in making a judgment regarding the operations of the organization. Consideration would also be given to how much of the profits was used for exempt purposes in proportion to how much was allowed to accumulate or was reinvested in the business venture. In general, an organization will probably not be "exclusively operated" for an exempt purpose if it conducts commercial activities in which large amounts of profits are generated and accumulated rather than used to further exempt purposes. On the other hand, if the profits are relatively small, or if even large amounts of profits are used to further exempt activities, the organization has a somewhat better chance of showing that it is "exclusively operated" for exempt purpose.

This concept was illustrated in *Presbyterian & Reform Publishing Company v. Commissioner,*[20] in which the tax-exempt status of a religious publishing company was upheld, despite the existence of a large amount of accumulated profits earned as a result of extensive commercial activity. The Third Circuit stated that a large accumulation of profits does not per se bar qualification of an organization for tax-exempt status. The court found that the large accumulation of profits indicated commercial viability, but gave latitude to the organization because the organization showed that the accumulated profits were to be used to acquire a new printing plant which would, in turn, further its exempt purpose.

Compare the result in *Presbyterian & Reform Publishing Company* with that in *Scripture Press* where the Court of Claims found the organization not "exclusively operated" for an exempt purpose because it had the capability to accumulate profits. In *Scripture Press* the court did not consider the purpose for which the profits would be used. Also compare *Federation Pharmacy Services, Inc.*, in which the Eighth Circuit found the organization not "exclusively operated" for an exempt purpose even though the commercial activity was carried on "at cost," and thus, the organization could never realize a profit.

A commercial activity will be viewed with a wider scope if the organization conducting the activity can establish that the activity is functionally related to its exempt purposes. This has been especially so in the case of organizations whose exempt purposes fall under the advancement of religion category. Courts have traditionally been reluctant to deny tax-exempt status to religious organizations on the basis of their religious teachings and beliefs, and have shown greater tolerance for commercial activities which function in furtherance of the organization's exempt purpose.

Although not as prevalant as in the case of "religious" organizations, there is some tolerance for functionally related commercial activities engaged in by other types of organizations. For example, in *Edward Orton Ceramic Foundation,*[21] the tax court held that the organization's manufacture of ceramic tiles did not destroy its exclusive operation for the exempt purpose of research in ceramic processes because the manufacture of the tiles (commercial activity) was not shown to be unrelated to the organization's exempt purpose. The decision was also based on an earlier decision by the tax court[22] in which it held that the profits obtained from the manufacturing activity did not destroy the Orton Foundation's tax-exempt status. In that instance the tax court considered that the organization limited itself to a 20 percent profit margin and also used most of the profits to fund its exempt purpose—research.

Finally, if a commercial activity provides no private benefit to the organization's shareholders or to any other individuals, there is an increased likelihood that the commercial activity could be found not to destroy the organization's tax-exempt status. It is clear that in determining whether an organization is operated exclusively for an exempt purpose, many factors are considered. The goal of any organization should be to maintain business activities, if at all, at a level that can be shown to be only incidental to its activities in furtherance of its exempt purpose. As business activities increase, an organization should at least take steps to ensure that profits are used in furtherance of its exempt purpose. Also, it is wise to at least keep any business activities functionally related to the organization's exempt purpose.

EXEMPT PURPOSES

The exempt purposes described in Section 501(c)(3) include (a) religious, (b) charitable, (c) scientific, (d) testing for public safety, (e) literary, (f) educational, and (g) prevention of cruelty to children and animals.[23] Because each of these purposes is an exempt purpose in itself, an organization may be exempt if it is organized and operated exclusively for any one or more of such purposes.[24] For this reason, if an organization is organized and operated for any one or more of such purposes, exemption will be granted to such organization regardless of the purposes specified in its application for exemption.[25] For example, if an organization claims exemption on the grounds that it is "educational," exemption will not be denied if, in fact, it is "charitable."[26]

Charitable Purpose

A charitable purpose is the first, and by far the most encompassing, exempt purpose listed under Section 501(c)(3). According to the Regulations, the term charitable is used in Section 501(c)(3) in its generally accepted legal sense and is, therefore, not to be construed as limited by the separate enumeration in Section 501(c)(3) of other tax-exempt purposes which may fall within the broad outlines of "charity" as developed by judicial decisions. The term charitable includes: relief of the poor and distressed or underprivileged; advancement of religion;

advancement of education; erection or maintenance of public buildings, monuments, or works; lessening of the burdens of government; and promotion of social welfare by organizations designed to accomplish any of the above purposes or to lessen neighborhood tensions, to eliminate prejudice and discrimination, to defend human and civil rights secured by law, or to combat community deterioration and juvenile delinquency.[27]

So long as an organization is not an "action" organization (i.e., a substantial part of its activities consists of attempting to influence legislation), it can qualify under Section 501(c)(3) even if, in carrying out its primary purpose, it advocates social or civic changes or presents an opinion on controversial issues with the intention of molding public opinion or creating public sentiment to an acceptance of its views.[28]

It is evident that a charitable purpose encompasses a wide variety of activities. The labeling of an activity as charitable in nature is always a question of the facts and circumstances, with specific attention given to the purpose for which it was organized. But, however broad the category may be, and however commendable the purpose, an organization will be granted tax-exempt status as a charitable organization only if it serves a public rather than a private interest. This concept is somewhat related to the concept of the prohibition against private inurement to an organization's shareholders or other individuals. It is, however, to be distinguished as a separate requirement.

Public Interest, Illegality, and Public Policy

The concept of a "public interest" means that the general public, rather than a small class of individuals, will benefit from the organization's activities. There is no specific number requirement placed on the "general public" requirement; however, it is clear that the greater the number of persons benefited, the easier it is to establish a public interest. The concept of "public interest" is not based entirely upon a tally of the number of persons benefiting. It is also based upon whether a "public good" is accomplished. This can be illustrated by Revenue Ruling 76-204.[29] In that ruling, an ecological group purchased ecologically significant lands and wished to preserve them in their natural state. The public, however, was excluded from the lands because public use would have destroyed the natural state of the lands. The ruling held that a public interest would be served in the protection of the natural environment. Here, it did not matter that the public was actually excluded from the lands; there was a "public good" to be found in the activity itself from which the public would benefit.

There are also prohibitions placed on the granting of tax-exempt status to any organization which is organized or operated for illegal purposes, or to an organization which attempts to carry out its charitable purpose by the use of illegal means. For example, an organization organized for the charitable purpose of preserving the ecological nature of certain land would not be granted tax-exempt status, or would be disqualified from such status if it attempted to prevent entrance to the lands by using physical force against those attempting to enter.

Additionally, tax-exempt status will not be granted to an organization which is organized or operated for purposes which are in violation of federal public policy. The most prevalent example of this is an organization which is organized or operated on a racially discriminatory basis. This rule has been extended to discrimination on the basis of ethnic origin, but has not been extended to discrimination on the basis of sex.

The issue of racial discrimination has been particularly prevalent in the area of private nonprofit schools which operate on a racially segregated basis. In 1971, as a result of a group of cases centered around Mississippi private schools operating on a racially discriminatory basis,[30] the IRS announced that it would refuse to grant tax-exempt status to private schools with a discriminatory admissions policy.[31] This policy was challenged by two schools, Goldsboro Christian School and Bob Jones University, both of which operated under racially discriminatory policies. They argued that their policy was religiously motivated and that under the First Amendment of the United States Constitution, they were entitled to exercise their beliefs even if against public policy. However, the United States Supreme Court disagreed.[32] The Court ruled that a racially discriminatory policy, even though religiously motivated, violated public policy, and therefore, barred tax-exempt status.[33]

Advancement of Religion, Education, or Science

Although separately enumerated as exempt purposes in and of themselves, religious, educational, and scientific purposes can overlap into the "charitable" category. This overlap occurs most often when an organization cannot meet all of the specific requirements necessary in order to establish itself as tax-exempt under the religious, educational, or scientific categories. This overlap also occurs when an organization provides a related service to a religious, educational, or scientific organization, but does not by itself meet the requirements of the separate category.

Hospitals

A nonprofit organization that provides hospital care promotes the health of the public, and can be recognized as a tax-exempt charitable organization. Exempt status as a hospital is dependent on the level of service given to the members of the community surrounding the hospital facility. This means that a tax-exempt hospital must make some provision for the care of those persons who are unable to pay all, or are able to pay only a portion, of the hospital fees. There is no specific level of free or below-cost care that a tax-exempt hospital must render; however, Revenue Ruling 69-545[34] makes it clear that the IRS regards as significant factors such as whether the hospital operates an emergency room which is open to all persons regardless of ability to pay and whether the hospital provides care to all those in the community who are unable to pay.

Basically, the IRS examines community benefit and community involvement. In this regard, a hospital or clinic established to provide specialized cosmetic surgery procedures to only those patients who could afford to pay the high medical costs and fees would not be granted tax-exempt status. This is because the hospital makes no provision for those unable to pay for services. On the other hand, if the hospital is established with the purpose of providing corrective cosmetic surgery at reduced cost, or at no cost to those who could not afford to pay, the hospital would have a greater chance of obtaining tax-exempt status. In this case, the hospital would be of benefit to the community as a whole and would make provisions for nonpaying patients.

Educational Purpose

An organization is dedicated to an educational purpose if it is engaged in the instruction or training of individuals for the purpose of improving or developing their capabilities.[35] An organization is also dedicated to an educational purpose if it is engaged in instructing the public on subjects useful to individuals and beneficial to the community.[36]

An educational organization can be thought of in the formal sense as a school, be it a primary or secondary school, a college, or a professional or trade school.[37] In the formal sense, such an organization would be characterized by a regularly scheduled curriculum, a regular faculty, and a regularly enrolled body of students in attendance at a place where the educational activities are regularly carried on.[38] On the other hand, an organization dedicated to educational purposes can be one whose activities consist of presenting public discussion groups, forums, panels, lectures, or other similar programs.[39] Such programs may also be presented on radio or television.[40] The presentation of television or radio correspondence instruction is also recognized as having an educational purpose.[41] Finally, museums, zoos, planetariums, symphony orchestras, and similar organizations are recognized as having an educational purpose.[42]

According to the Regulations, it is permissible for an educational organization to advocate a particular position or viewpoint.[43] This is the case so long as the organization promoting the position or viewpoint presents a sufficiently full and fair exposition of the pertinent facts so that an individual or the public would be able to form an independent opinion or conclusion.[44] An organization would not be considered educational if its principal function is merely to present an unsupported opinion.[45]

Basing its position on Regulation Section 1.501(c)(3)-1(d)(3), the IRS has always been concerned with the "method" used by an organization to communicate its viewpoint or position to others rather than on the actual viewpoint or position itself.[46] However, historically, the application of the Regulation was rather troublesome in that it created the opportunity for public officials to impose their own preconceptions and beliefs in the determination of whether a particular viewpoint or position was educational.

As a result of several years of uncertainty in the application of the regulation, in 1980 it was challenged and ultimately found invalid in *Big Mama Rag v. U.S.*[47] The court held that the Regulation was invalid because it felt that its provisions were unconstitutionally vague. This vagueness, in turn, hindered the ability of public officials to judge an organization's beliefs and purposes with the disinterested neutrality necessary to a fair determination of an educational purpose.

A second case challenged the constitutionality of the regulation in 1983. In that case, *National Alliance v. U.S.*,[48] the court did not reach the question of the constitutionality of the regulation. However, the court did uphold the position of the IRS that the organization involved did not have an educational purpose. In so holding, the court adopted the "methodology test" which had been proposed by the IRS in applying the regulation

The methodology test is used by the IRS to evaluate the educational purpose of any organization that advocates a particular viewpoint or position. This test examines the method used by the organization in advocating its position, rather than the position itself, as the standard for such evaluation.[49] The methodology test was set out in a 1986 Revenue Procedure which stated that the test reflects the "long-standing" position of the Service.[50] The Revenue Procedure does not amend, nor does it withdraw the challenged regulation; rather, it sets out a detailed list of factors used by the IRS in determining whether an "advocacy" organization has an educational purpose.

The Revenue Procedure states that, in addition to meeting all other requirements for exemption under Section 501(c)(3), to be considered educational, an organization must provide a factual foundation for the viewpoint or position which it advocates and must also provide a development from the relevant facts which would materially aid a listener or reader in a learning process. The Revenue Procedure also lists several factors, the presence of which would indicate that the methods used by the organization to advocate its viewpoints or positions are not educational. These factors are: (1) a significant portion of the organization's communications consists of the presentation of viewpoints or positions unsupported by facts; (2) the facts that purport to support the viewpoints or position are distorted; (3) the organization's presentations make substantial use of inflammatory and disparaging terms and express conclusions based more on strong emotional feelings than on objective evaluations; and (4) the approach used by the organization in its presentations is not aimed at developing an understanding on the part of the audience or readership because it does not consider their background or training in the subject matter. Finally, the Revenue Procedure points out that the IRS will examine all the facts and circumstances in making its determination in regard to the educational nature of an organization. Therefore, it is possible that, in limited situations, the facts and circumstances would prove an organization's advocacy to be educational even though one or more of the above-listed factors are present.[51]

Scientific Purpose

The Regulations define the term "scientific" in terms of "research." However, it should be noted that an organization devoted to research may or may not be scientific within the meaning of Section 501(c)(3) and that the meaning of "scientific" embraces activities beyond the narrow category of "research." The Regulations make it clear that the term "research" is not synonymous with the term "scientific";[52] however, research is probably the most common type of scientific purpose.

In order for a scientific research organization to qualify for tax-exempt status as an organization having a scientific purpose, the research activities must be conducted for the public interest and in furtherance of scientific purpose.[53] This means that research activities ordinarily carried on incidental to commercial or industrial operations would not qualify as carried on in the public interest.[54] Such research would include the ordinary testing or inspection of materials or products, or the designing or construction of equipment or buildings.[55] Such activities would be considered to be carried on for private, rather than public, interest because they are connected to commercially viable businesses.

Scientific research will be regarded as carried on in the public interest if the results of the research are made available to the public on a non-discriminatory basis. Such results would include patents, copyrights, processes, or formulae resulting from such research.[56] Scientific research will be regarded as carried on in the public interest if such research is performed for the United States, or any of its agencies or instrumentalities, or for a state or political subdivision of the United States.[57] Finally, scientific research will be regarded as carried on in the public interest if such research is directed toward benefiting the public.[58]

For example, scientific research benefits the public if it is carried on for the purpose of aiding in the scientific education of college or university students; carried on for the purpose of obtaining scientific information which is published in a treatise, thesis, trade publication, or in any other form that is available to the interested public; carried on for the purpose of discovering a cure for a disease; or carried on for the purpose of aiding a community or geographical area by attracting new industry to the community or area.[59] Research which benefits the public will be regarded as carried on in the public interest even though the research is performed pursuant to a contract or agreement under which the sponsor of the research has the right to obtain ownership or control of any patents, copyrights, processes, or formulae resulting from the research.[60]

An organization will not qualify as a scientific research organization under Section 501(c)(3) if it performs research only for persons who are, directly or indirectly, its creators or if the organization retains, directly or indirectly, more than an insubstantial portion of the patents, copyrights, processes, or formulae resulting from its research and does not make such patents, copyrights, processes, or formulae available to the public.[61] Availability to the public must be provided on a nondiscriminatory basis.[62]

Again, the Regulations fail to define the term "insubstantial." However, the regulations do provide that, so long as the scientific research is being provided for the government, or is carried on in the public interest for the purpose of benefiting the public in one of the ways listed in the Regulations, the exclusive right to the use of the resulting patent, copyright, process, or formula may be granted to a private individual if the granting of such exclusive right is the only practical way to utilize the patent, copyright, process, or formula for public benefit.[63]

An organization (including a college, university, or hospital) which engages in research activities which are not in furtherance of tax-exempt purpose as described in Section 501(c)(3), will not be precluded from qualification for tax-exempt status under Section 501(c)(3) so long as the organization meets the organizational test and is not operated for the primary purpose of engaging in such research.[64] Any income resulting from such research may, however, be subject to tax on unrelated business income.[65]

An organization engaging in research and wishing to obtain tax-exempt status under the scientific category of Section 501(c)(3) should submit the following in its application to the IRS: (1) an explanation of the nature of the research; (2) a brief description of research projects completed or in which the organization is presently engaged; (3) how and by whom research projects are determined and selected; (4) whether the organization has or is contemplating contracted or sponsored research, and if so, names of any past sponsors or grantors, terms of grants or contracts, and copies of any executed grants or contracts; (5) statement of disposition made or to be made of research results, and whether preference has been or will be given to any individual or organization either as to results or time of release; (6) names of those who will retain ownership of any patents, copyrights, processes, or formulae which may result from the research; and (7) a copy of publications or other media showing reports of the organization's research activities.[66]

Religious Purposes

Although there has been a great deal of litigation regarding the tax-exempt status of organizations claiming to be organized and operated for a religious purpose, tax law, including the Statute and the Regulations, does not offer a decisive definition of the term "religious." Likewise, neither the IRS nor the courts has been forthcoming with such a definition. This lack of set guidelines is primarily the result of the right to religious freedom as guaranteed by the Constitution of the United States. The determination of whether an organization is organized and operated for a religious purpose is, then, a matter of examination of the facts and circumstances surrounding that particular organization.

Tax-exempt status based on a religious purpose can be divided into two areas of meaning. The first is in the formal sense of a church; the second is in the less formal sense of a religious organization. The distinction is that all religious organizations do not rise to the level of qualification as a church.

In determining whether an organization is organized and operated for a religious purpose, the IRS maintains two basic guidelines. First, the particular religious belief of the organization must be truly and sincerely held. Second, the practices and rituals associated with the organization's religious belief or creed must not be illegal or contrary to clearly defined public policy.[67] The IRS will not question the religious doctrine of an organization beyond these two set guidelines. However, the IRS has other methods of attack on so-called religious organizations such as questioning possible private inurement.

If it is possible for an organization to so qualify, there are several advantages to being categorized as a church or church-related auxiliary. First, a church or church-related auxiliary is not required to apply for recognition of tax-exempt status, although it is required to meet all of the requirements of Section 501(c)(3).[68] Many churches do, however, apply for formal recognition as a safeguard for their contributors to ensure that their contributions will be deductible up to the maximum limitation of 50 percent of income. Second, a church or church-related auxiliary is automatically classified as a "public charity" rather than as a private foundation, thus avoiding the restrictions and excise taxes placed on private foundations.[69] Third, a church or church-related auxiliary is not required to file the annual informational return (Form 990) required of other tax-exempt organizations.[70] Finally, a church or church-related auxiliary is granted special concessions if an audit is conducted by the IRS.[71]

A church-related auxiliary is a separate organization affiliated with a church, but able to qualify on its own for tax-exempt status as a religious organization. The principal activity of such an organization must be religious oriented.

The single attempt by the regulations to define the term "religious" is found within the unrelated business income sections. The definition describes a church as an organization whose duties include the ministration of sacerdotal functions and the conduct of religious worship.[72] There is no attempt to further explain exactly what constitutes "sacerdotal functions" or "religious worship." In an attempt to aid in identifying a "church," the Internal Revenue Manual lists several characteristics which the IRS applies in making its determination. An organization does not have to exhibit every characteristic, nor does the IRS place particular importance or emphasis on any one characteristic. Rather, each organization is examined for its individual merits. The characteristics are as follows: a distinct legal existence, a recognized creed and form of worship, a definite and distinct ecclesiastical government, a formal code of doctrine and discipline, a distinct religious history, a membership not associated with any other church or denomination, an organization of ordained ministers, these ordained ministers having been selected after completing prescribed studies, a literature of its own, established places of worship, an established congregation, regular religious services, religious education for the young, and schools for the preparation of its ministers.[73]

Because the IRS is reluctant to challenge a religious organization on the basis of its beliefs and doctrines, the IRS has looked to other areas in which so-called religious organizations or churches abuse the privilege of their tax-exempt status. One of the most prevalent of these problem areas is that of private inurement. A somewhat common occurrence on this theme is when a person establishes a "church," appoints himself or herself minister, and assigns all of his or her income to the church. The church then pays all expenses of the minister. The minister then asserts that he or she had no personal income tax liability and was not subject to withholding. The IRS has routinely disqualified such organizations as "churches" due to private inurement. Additionally, the IRS has questioned excessive salary payments to a church minister as a potential private inurement problem. The general approach is to examine the amount of time and effort spent by the minister in fulfilling his or her duties. There is no prohibition against the payment of a reasonable salary either to the minister or to church workers, and such payment will not be construed as private inurement.

ACTION ORGANIZATIONS

An organization will not qualify for tax-exempt status under Section 501(c)(3) if more than an insubstantial part of its activities is devoted to attempting to influence legislation by propaganda or otherwise.[74] Such an organization would not be organized and operated exclusively for exempt purposes, and would be classified as an "action" organization.[75] An action organization, therefore, is one which devotes a substantial part of its activities to attempting to influence legislation by propaganda or otherwise.[76]

An organization will be regarded as attempting to influence legislation if the organization contacts, or urges the public to contact, members of a legislative body for the purpose of proposing, supporting, or opposing legislation; or, if it advocates the adoption or rejection of legislation.[77] The term "legislation" includes action by Congress, a state legislature, a local council or similar governing body, or by the public in a referendum, initiative, constitutional amendment, or similar procedure. An organization may advocate the adoption or rejection of legislation without jeopardizing its ability to meet the operational test, so long as it is done as an insubstantial part of its activities.[78]

Certain activities are not considered attempts to influence legislation. These include:

1. Making available the results of nonpartisan analysis, study or research;

2. Providing technical advice or assistance (where such advice would otherwise constitute the influencing of legislation) to a governmental body in response to a written request by the governmental body;
3. Appearing before, or communicating with, any legislative body with respect to a possible decision of the body which might affect the existence of the organization, its powers and duties, its tax-exempt status, or the deduction of contributions to the organization;
4. Communicating with bona fide members of the organization regarding legislation or proposed legislation of direct interest to the organization and its members unless the communications directly encourage the members to influence legislation or directly encourage the members to encourage nonmembers to influence legislation;
5. Communicating with a government official or employee for any purpose other than attempting to influence legislation.[79]

An organization is also classified as an action organization if it directly or indirectly participates in or intervenes in any political campaign on behalf of or in opposition to any candidate for public office. These activities include the publication or distribution of written or printed statements and making oral statements on behalf of or in opposition to that candidate.[80]

An organization will also be classified as an action organization if its main or primary objective may be attained only by legislation or a defeat of proposed legislation, and if it advocates, or campaigns for, the attainment of that main or primary objective. These activities should be distinguished from permissible activities of engaging in nonpartisan analysis, study, or research and making the results thereof available to the public. Whether an organization has such objectives and conducts such activities is determined by an examination of the surrounding facts and circumstances.[81]

Neither the code nor the regulations indicates how much activity to influence legislation will be considered a "substantial" part of an organization's activities. This creates a problem for any organization which has an interest in influencing legislation, but wants to keep such activities an insubstantial part of its overall activities so as not to jeopardize its tax-exempt status. An organization in that position may benefit from making an election under Section 501(h) to be subject to a precise test which quantifies a limit on the amount of expenditures which may be made for influencing legislation without jeopardizing its tax-exempt status.

Any public charity (except a church, a convention or association of churches, or a member of an affiliated group of organizations which include a church) may make the election under Section 501(h).[82] The test under Section 501(h) sets a limit on the dollar amount that can be expended for the purpose of influencing legislation by communicating with legislators or other government officials who participate in formulating legislation (lobbying activities) and through attempts to affect the opinions of the general public with regard to legislation (grass roots lobbying).[83] An electing organization must make an annual calculation of its "lobbying nontaxable amount" and its "grass roots nontaxable amount." An electing organization that keeps its lobbying expenditures below these two limits will not jeopardize its tax-exempt status, nor become subject to a special excise tax which is levied upon electing organizations that exceed the limits.[84]

The lobbying nontaxable amount for any organization for any taxable year is expressed as a percentage of exempt purpose expenditures for the year. The expenditure limitations are 20 percent of the exempt purpose expenditures up to $500,000; $100,000 plus 15 percent of the excess of the exempt purpose expenditures over $500,000 up to $1,000,000; $175,000 plus 10 percent of the excess of the exempt purpose expenditures over $1,000,000 up to $1,500,000; or $225,000 plus 5 percent of the excess of the exempt purpose expenditures over $1,500,000.[85] The lobbying nontaxable amount may never exceed $1,000,000. The grass roots nontaxable amount for any organization for any taxable year is 25 percent of the lobbying nontaxable amount for that year.[86]

"Exempt purpose expenditures" means, for purposes of the calculations, the total of the organization's charitable expenditures (including religious, charitable, and educational) and lobbying expenditures for the year.[87]

An organization that makes expenditures to influence legislation which exceed its lobbying nontaxable amount or its grass roots nontaxable amount will be subject to an excise tax. The excise tax imposed is 25 percent of the greater of two amounts: the excess of the lobbying expenditures over the lobbying nontaxable amount, or the excess of the grass roots expenditures over the grass roots nontaxable amount.[88]

However, an electing organization will lose its tax-exempt status if its lobbying expenditures normally exceed 150 percent of the lobbying nontaxable amount for the year or if its grass roots lobbying expenditures normally exceed 150 percent of its grass roots nontaxable amount for the year.[89] (Much of the uncertainty regarding the definition of the terms which appear in Section 501(h) has been addressed pursuant to final Regulations that became effective for taxable years beginning after 31 August 1990.)

For tax years prior to 1977, a 501(c)(3) organization that lost its exemption because of excess lobbying activity could be reclassified as a 501(c)(4) organization which is not restricted as to lobbying activities. However, for years after 1976, Section 504 prohibits a 501(c)(3) organization from being reclassified as a 501(c)(4) organization if the 501(c)(3) organization loses its tax-exempt status because it, as a substantial part of its activities, carries on propaganda or attempts to influence legislation or participates or intervenes in any political campaign on behalf of, or in opposition to, a candidate for public office.

FEEDER ORGANIZATIONS

Prior to the Revenue Act of 1950, it was possible for a tax-exempt organization to establish a separate organization which would carry on a business for profit as a substantial part of its activities. This profit was then paid over to the tax-exempt organization, thereby allowing it to retain its tax-exempt status and still benefit from a business operation which it could not conduct as part of its own exempt activities. The underlying notion was that the "destination" of the income was for a tax-exempt purpose, so the "source" of the income was not really important.

In order to end this ability of tax-exempt organizations to circumvent the rules regarding the prohibition on engaging in a business activity as a substantial part of their activities by having a separate organization conduct the business for them, Congress enacted the "feeder organization" provisions.

The feeder organization provisions state that in the case of any organization operated for the primary purpose of carrying on a trade or business for profit, exemption is not allowed under Section 501 simply because the profits are payable to an exempt organization.[90] A review of all of the facts and circumstances is necessary to determine whether the primary purpose of the organization is to carry on a trade or business for profit.[91]

A subsidiary organization of a tax-exempt organization may retain its tax-exempt status if its activities are an integral part of the exempt activities of the parent organization. This is so even if profits result to the subsidiary from its dealings with the parent organization.[92] On the other hand, the subsidiary would not retain its tax-exempt status if it is operated for the primary purpose of carrying on a trade or business which would be an unrelated trade or business if regularly carried on by the parent organization. For example, a subsidiary of a tax-exempt educational organization would retain its tax-exempt status if it is operated for the sole purpose of furnishing electric power to the parent organization for use in carrying on its educational activities. However, if the subsidiary organization is operated primarily for the purpose of furnishing electric power to consumers rather than its parent organization (and the parent's tax-exempt subsidiary organizations), it would not retain its tax-exempt status because the business would be an unrelated trade or business if regularly carried on by the parent organization.[93]

NOTES

1. IRC Sec. 170(b).
2. Reg. Sec. 1.501(c)(3)-1(b)(6).
3. Reg. Sec. 1.501(c)(3)-1(b)(1)(i)(a) and (b).
4. Reg. Sec. 1.501(c)(3)-1(b)(2).
5. Reg. Sec. 1.501(c)(3)-1(b)(1)(ii).
6. Id.
7. Reg. Sec. 1.501(c)(3)-1(b)(5).
8. Id.
9. Reg. Sec. 1.501(c)(3)-(1)(b)(1)(i)(b) and (iii).
10. Reg. Sec. 1.501(c)(3)-(1)(b)(3).
11. Reg. Sec. 1.501(c)(3)-(1)(b)(4).
12. Id.
13. Reg. Sec. 1.501(c)(3)-1(b)(5).
14. Colorado State Chiropractic Society, 93 T.C. 39 (1989).
15. Reg. Sec. 1.501(c)(3)-1(c)(1), (2), and (3).
16. Reg. Sec. 1.501(c)(3)-1(c)(1).
17. Paul E. Treusch, *Tax-Exempt Charitable Organizations,* 3rd ed. 1988, citing INT. REV. MANUAL 7(10).

18. 285 F.2d 800 (Ct. C1. 1961).
19. 72 T.C. 687 (1979), aff'd, 625 F.2d 804 (8th Cir. 1980).
20. 743 F.2d 148 (3rd Cir. 1984), rev'g, 79 T.C. 1070 (1982).
21. 56 T.C. 147 (1971).
22. T.C. 533, aff'd, 173 F.2d 483 (6th Cir. 1949).
23. Reg. Sec. 1.501(c)(3)-1(d)(1)(i).
24. Reg. Sec. 1.501(c)(3)-1(d)(1)(iii).
25. Id.
26. Id.
27. Reg. Sec. 1.501(c)(3)-1(d)(2).
28. Id.
29. 1976-1 C.B. 152.
30. Green v. Kennedy, 309 F. Supp. 1127 (D.C. Cir. 1970); Green v. Connally, 330 F. Supp. 1150 (D.C. Cir. 1971); Coit v. Green, 404 U.S. 997 (1971).
31. Rev. Rul. 71-447, 1971-2 C.B. 230.
32. Bob Jones University and Goldsboro Christian School, 461 U.S. 574 (1983).
33. Id.
34. 1969-2 C.B. 117.
35. Reg. Sec. 1.501(c)(3)-1(d)(3)(i)(a).
36. Reg. Sec. 1.501(c)(3)-1(d)(3)(i)(b).
37. Reg. Sec. 1.501(c)(3)-1(d)(3)(ii) ex. 1.
38. Id.
39. Reg. Sec. 1.501(c)(3)-1(d)(3)(ii) ex. 2.
40. Id.
41. Reg. Sec. 1.501(c)(3)-1(d)(3)(ii) ex. 3.
42. Reg. Sec. 1.501(c)(3)-1(d)(3)(ii) ex. 4.
43. Reg. Sec. 1.501(c)(3)-1(d)(3).
44. Id.
45. Id.
46. Rev. Proc. 86-43, 1986-2 C.B. 729.
47. 631 F.2d 1030 (D.C. Cir. 1980).
48. 710 F.2d 868 (D.C. Cir. 1983).
49. Rev. Proc. 86-43, 1986-2 C.B. 729.
50. Id.
51. Id.
52. Reg. Sec. 1.501(c)(3)-1(d)(5)(i).
53. Id.
54. Reg. Sec. 1.501(c)(3)-1(d)(5)(ii).
55. Id.
56. Reg. Sec. 1.501(c)(3)-1(d)(5)(iii)(a).
57. Reg. Sec. 1.501(c)(3)-1(d)(5)(iii)(b).

58. Reg. Sec. 1.501(c)(3)-1(d)(5)(iii)(c).
59. Reg. Sec. 1.501(c)(3)-1(d)(5)(iii)(c)(1), (2), (3), and (4).
60. Reg. Sec. 1.501(c)(3)-1(d)(5)(iii)(c).
61. Reg. Sec. 1.501(c)(3)-1(d)(5)(iv)(a) and (b).
62. Reg. Sec. 1.501(c)(3)-1(d)(5)(iv)(b).
63. Id.
64. Reg. Sec. 1.501(c)(3)-1(e).
65. The tax on unrelated business income will be discussed in Chapter 4.
66. IRS Publication 557.
67. Id.
68. IRC Sec. 508(c)(1)(A).
69. IRC Sec. 509(a)(1).
70. IRC Sec. 6033(a)(2)(A)(i).
71. IRC 7611.
72. Reg. Sec. 1.501-2(a)(3)(ii).
73. Treusch, p. 106.
74. Reg. Sec. 1.501(c)(3)-1(c)(3).
75. Reg. Sec. 1.501(c)(3)-1(c)(3)(i).
76. Reg. Sec. 1.501(c)(3)-1(c)(3)(ii).
77. Reg. Sec. 1.501(c)(3)-1(c)(3)(ii)(a) and (b).
78. Reg. Sec. 1.501(c)(3)-1(c)(3).
79. IRC Sec. 4911(d).
80. Reg. Sec. 1.501(c)(3)-1(c)(3)(iii).
81. Reg. Sec. 1.501(c)(3)-1(c)(3)(iv).
82. IRC Sec. 501(h)(3), (4), and (5).
83. IRC Sec. 501(h)(2)(A) and (C); IRC Sec. 4911(d)(1)(A) and (B).
84. IRC Sec. 4911(a)(1).
85. IRC Sec. 4911(c)(2).
86. Id.
87. IRC Sec. 4911(e)(1).
88. IRC Sec. 4911(a)(1) and (b)(1) and (2).
89. IRC Sec. 501(h)(1) and (2).
90. Reg. Sec. 1.502-1(a).
91. Id.
92. Reg. Sec. 1.502-1(b).
93. Id. For an expanded view of many of the subjects contained in this chapter see Treusch, note 17.

3

Other Tax-Exempt Organizations

Several types of organizations qualify for tax-exempt status granted by Section 501(a) of the Internal Revenue Code of 1986. The types of organizations are widely varied, ranging from an instrumentality of the United States to a social club. Descriptions of the various organizations appear below.

INSTRUMENTALITIES OF THE UNITED STATES

Organizations exempt under this category are governmentally incorporated instrumentalities of the United States.[1] An example of such an organization is a governmentally controlled educational institution such as a college or university.

TITLE HOLDING COMPANIES

Title-Holding Companies Under Section 501(c)(2)

Tax-exempt status is granted under Section 501(c)(2) to a corporation which is organized for the exclusive purpose of holding title to property, collecting the income therefrom, and turning over the income collected, less expenses, to another exempt organization. If a title-holding company engages in any other type of business, it will lose its exempt status.[2] A title-holding company would also lose its exempt status if it failed to turn over its entire net income, less expenses, to another exempt organization, choosing instead to accumulate such income in its own business.[3]

In applying for tax-exempt status, a title holding company must submit Form 1024 to the IRS. The title-holding company must also submit a copy of its corporate charter which appropriately limits its activities to those enumerated under Section 501(c)(2). A title-holding company must also submit evidence necessary to determine the status of the organization for which title is held if such organization has not been specifically notified in writing by the IRS that it is exempt.[4]

Title-Holding Companies Under Section 501(c)(25)

A title-holding company organized under Section 501(c)(2) must limit the distribution of its income to only one tax-exempt organization. A title-holding company organized under Section 501(c)(25) is permitted to make such distributions to as many as thirty-five other tax-exempt organizations.

A 501(c)(25) organization must be organized as a corporation or trust which has no more than thirty-five shareholders or beneficiaries, which has only one class of stock or beneficial interest, and which is organized for the exclusive purpose of acquiring and holding title to real property, collecting the income from that property, and remitting the entire amount of the income, less expenses, to one or more eligible tax-exempt organizations that are shareholders of such organization or beneficiaries of such trust.[5]

In order to qualify as a Section 501(c)(25) investment, real property must be held directly and may not be held as a tenant in common (or other similar interest).[6] The term "real property" does include personal property which is leased under (or in connection with) a lease of real property, provided that the rent for the taxable year attributable to the personal property is not greater than 15 percent of the total rent for the taxable year attributable to both the real and the personal property.[7]

Permissible shareholders or beneficiaries of a Section 501(c)(25) title-holding company are a qualified pension, profit-sharing, or stock bonus plan; a governmental pension plan; the United States, any state or political subdivision thereof, or any governmental agency or instrumentality; and any tax-exempt organization described in Section

501(c)(3) such as a charitable, educational, or religious organization.[8]

A Section 501(c)(25) title-holding company does not have to be organized by its shareholders or beneficiaries, but may be organized by investment advisors.[9] However, a title-holding corporation or trust must permit its shareholders or beneficiaries to dismiss the investment advisor, following reasonable notice, upon a majority vote of the shareholders or beneficiaries, and also to terminate their interest in the corporation or trust by either or both of two methods: the sale or exchange of their stock or trust interest to another eligible shareholder or beneficiary (so long as the sale or exchange does not increase the number of shareholders or beneficiaries in the corporation or trust above thirty-five), or the redemption of their stock or trust interest by the corporation or trust after ninety days notice to the corporation or trust.[10]

CIVIC LEAGUES AND SOCIAL WELFARE ORGANIZATIONS

An organization operated exclusively for the promotion of social welfare may be tax-exempt under Section 501(c)(4). An organization is operated exclusively for the promotion of social welfare if it is engaged primarily in promoting the common good and general welfare of the people of the community with the primary purpose of achieving civic betterment and social improvement.[11] However, a social welfare organization may not be organized or operated for profit.[12]

A social welfare organization may not intervene or participate either directly or indirectly in a political campaign on behalf of, or in opposition to, any candidate for public office.[13] Nor may a social welfare organization operate, as its primary activity, a social club for the benefit, pleasure, or recreation of its members.[14]

A social welfare organization is much like a charitable organization exempt under Section 501(c)(3). In fact, if a social welfare organization is not an action organization (which attempts to influence legislation by lobbying activities), it could qualify as a charitable organization under Section 501(c)(3).[15] A social welfare organization can be thought of as a ''small-scale'' charitable organization because its focus is to benefit the people of the community, while the focus of a charitable organization is to benefit the general public. However, the important difference between a social welfare organization and a charitable organization is that a social welfare organization is permitted to be, to some extent, an action organization. This means that a social welfare organization may engage in lobbying activities without jeopardizing its tax-exempt status. This may be an important consideration to an organization making its initial determination as to the type of exemption for which it will apply. The drawback in choosing to be a social welfare organization instead of a charitable organization is that contributions made to a social welfare organization do not provide the donor with a charitable contribution deduction as does a contribution to a charitable organization.[16]

An example of an organization which was granted tax-exempt status as a social welfare organization is an organization which was formed to promote the common good and welfare of the general public through the presentation at legislative and administrative hearings on tax matters, of views directed at the improvement of the tax system.[17]

To apply for tax-exempt status under Section 501(c)(4), an organization must submit Form 1024 to the IRS. The organization must indicate in its application that it is a nonprofit organization, organized to bring about common good and general welfare to the people of the the community.

LABOR, AGRICULTURAL, AND HORTICULTURAL ORGANIZATIONS

To qualify for tax-exempt status under Section 501(c)(5), labor, agricultural, or horticultural organizations must have as their objective the betterment of the conditions of workers, the improvement of the grade of their products, and the development of a higher degree of efficiency in their respective occupations.[18] Additionally, no net earnings may inure to the benefit of any individual member of a labor, agricultural, or horticultural organization.[19] Contributions made to such organizations do not entitle the donor to a deduction for a charitable contribution.

A labor organization is usually in the form of a labor union which is organized to protect and promote the interests of labor in connection with employment. It is especially important in this context to guard against private inurement to individual members of tax-exempt labor unions. The benefit derived by each individual member must come from the overall benefit derived by the fact that the individual is a member of the larger group. For example, as a "minor" part of its activities, a labor organization exempt under Section 501(c)(5), and formed to promote the welfare of law enforcement officers, provided funds for legal counsel to individual officers when legal action was brought against them in connection with the performance of their official duties. This was found to be an appropriate activity because legal action brought against law enforcement officers tends to disrupt working conditions and discourages such officials from fulfilling their responsibilities. Providing legal assistance to those individual officers, although technically a private inurement, tends to improve the conditions of employment for the group as a whole and, therefore, does not destroy the organization's tax-exempt status.[20]

Application for tax-exempt status as a labor, agricultural, or horticultural organization is made by submitting Form 1024 to the IRS. The organization must also include in its application organizational documents which outline the organization's exempt purposes and which state that no net earnings will inure to the benefit of any individual member.

BUSINESS LEAGUES

A business league, which is in the same general class as a chamber of commerce or board of trade, is an association of persons having some common business interest. The purpose of a business league must be the promotion of such common business interest; a business league may not engage in a regular business ordinarily carried on for profit.[21] The key to exemption as a business league is the promotion of an industry as a whole, such as the improvement of business conditions of one or more lines of business, as distinguished from the performance of a particular service for individual persons.[22] For example, an association of dairy farmers could promote the use of dairy products, but could not promote the use of XYZ brand of dairy products.

A business league is not permitted to have excess business activities or to carry on any type of business having commercial viability, even though the business is conducted on a cooperative basis or produces only enough income to be self-sustaining. Such business activity destroys tax exemption under this category.[23] A business league must be supported only by membership dues and assessments, and by income from substantially related activities.

There is no express limitation on the ability of a business league to engage in political activity. Therefore, a business league would not lose its exempt status under Section 501(c)(6) if it engaged in political activities or lobbying activities. However, dues and assessments paid by members of a business league are deductible to the member only in proportion to that amount of the membership dues used for lobbying activities with regard to matters which directly affect or are of benefit to the industry represented by the business league. Such activities include expenses which are attributable to appearance before, submission of statements to, or sending communications to members of legislative bodies with respect to legislation (or proposed legislation) of direct interest to the member, and communications of information between the member and the organization with respect to their proposing, supporting, or opposing legislation of direct interest to either the organization or to a member.[24] No deduction is allowed for dues and assessments used for expenditures for participation in or intervention in a political campaign on behalf of any candidate for public office, or in connection with any attempt to influence the general public or segments thereof with respect to legislative matters (grass roots lobbying), elections, or referenda.

Contributions to a business league do not entitle the donor to a deduction for a charitable contribution. However, such contributions may be deductible as a trade or business expense if they are ordinary and necessary in the conduct of the taxpayer donor's business.[25]

An organization may apply for tax-exempt status as a Section 501(c)(6) business league by submitting Form 1024 to the IRS. The application and organizational documents must indicate that no part of the organization's net earnings will inure to the benefit of any private shareholder or individual, and that it is not organized for profit or to engage in an activity ordinarily carried on for profit.

SOCIAL CLUBS

In order to qualify for tax-exempt status under Section 501(c)(7), a social club must:

1. Be organized and operated exclusively for pleasure, recreation, and other nonprofitable purposes, and substantially all of its activities must be devoted to such exempt purposes;[26]
2. Be supported solely by membership fees, dues, and assessments;[27]
3. Not allow any part of its net earnings to inure to the benefit of any private shareholder or individual;[28]

4. Not maintain any written policy statement which provides for discrimination against any person on the basis of race, color, or religion.[29]

The focus of the activities of a social club must be directed toward its members. Unlike other tax-exempt organizations which focus on providing benefits to the general public, a social club is not permitted to provide benefits to the general public. This is because in so doing, unpermitted private inurement may result to members of the social club. For example, if a social club opened its pool or restaurant facilities to the general public, profits realized could defray costs and expenses and private benefit could result to club members in the form of reduced membership fees.

There is also focus on personal contact, commingling, and fellowship among members of the social club. Although fellowship does not have to exist among all members of the social club, the group as a whole must be bound together by the common objective of pleasure, recreation, and other nonprofitable purposes. In other words, activities must be conducted in a collective sense. Additionally, the social club must place limitations on admission to membership which are consistent with the character of the club.[30]

A social club that engages in business such as making its social and recreational facilities available to the general public is not organized and operated exclusively for pleasure, recreation, and other nonprofitable purposes.[31] Solicitation, by advertisement or otherwise, for public patronage of its facilities is prima facie evidence that the social club is engaging in business and is not being operated exclusively for an exempt purpose.[32] However, the requirement that substantially all of a social club's activities must be devoted to exempt purposes is met if at least 65 percent of its gross receipts are derived from exempt sources. This means that up to 35 percent of a social club's gross receipts, including investment income, may be derived from sources outside of its membership without jeopardizing its exempt status. Of that 35 percent, not more than 15 percent of the gross receipts may be derived from the use of the club's facilities or services by the general public or from other activities not in furtherance of the social or recreational purposes of its members.[33] Income derived from the use of the facilities by guests is not considered income from the general public. For example, if a social club derived 10 percent of its gross receipts from nonmembers (10 percent being less than the 15 percent limit), it could derive up to 25 percent of its gross receipts from investment income without losing its tax-exempt status.

If a social club derives more than 35 percent of its gross receipts from nonmembership sources, the excess may be justified by an examination of all of the facts and circumstances. If the excess cannot be justified, the social club would lose its tax-exempt status.[34]

Gross receipts are receipts from normal and usual activities of the social club including charges, admissions, membership fees, dues, assessments, investment income, and normal recurring capital gains on investments. Initiation fees and capital contributions are excluded. Unusual receipts, such as from the sale of its clubhouse, are not included in gross receipts or in figuring the percentage limitations.

A social club can lose its exemption for any taxable year if, at any time during that year, the charter, bylaws, or other governing instrument or any written policy statement contains a provision which provides for discrimination against any person on the basis of race, color, or religion.[35] The restriction on religious discrimination does not apply to an auxiliary of a tax-exempt fraternal benefit society described in Section 501(c)(8) if it limits its members to a particular religion; nor does the restriction apply to a social club which in good faith limits its membership to the members of a particular religion in order to further the teachings or principles of that religion, and not to exclude individuals of a particular race or color.[36]

Contributions made to a social club do not entitle the donor to a charitable contribution deduction. Application for exemption as a social club is made by submitting Form 1024 to the IRS. Evidence should be presented to show the personal contact and fellowship among members and the limitations on admission to membership consistent with the character of the social club.

FRATERNAL BENEFICIARY SOCIETY AND DOMESTIC FRATERNAL SOCIETIES

A fraternal beneficiary society is a fraternal organization which operates under the lodge system, or for the exclusive benefit of the members of a fraternal organization which is itself operating under the lodge system, and provides for the payment of life, sick, accident, or other benefits to the members of such society or their dependents.[37] The benefits offered by the society must be limited to members and their dependents, and all members must be eligible to receive the benefits offered. However, it is not necessary for every member to be covered by the benefit program.

Operating under a lodge system means conducting activities under a system of organization comprised of largely self-governing local branch organizations which have been chartered by a parent organization.[38]

A domestic fraternal society is the same type of organization as a fraternal beneficiary society except that a domestic fraternal society does not provide for the payment of life, sick, accident, or other benefits to its members or their dependents.[39] A domestic fraternal society must operate under the lodge system and must devote its net earnings exclusively to religious, charitable, scientific, literary, educational, and fraternal purposes.[40]

Contributions made to both a fraternal beneficiary society and to a domestic fraternal society are tax deductible to the donor if the contribution is used exclusively for religious, charitable, scientific, literary, or educational purposes, or for the prevention of cruelty to children or animals. Both types of organization may apply for tax-exempt status by filing Form 1024 with the IRS. However, a domestic fraternal society must state that it does not provide for the payment of life, sick, accident, or other benefits to its members.[41]

EMPLOYEES' ASSOCIATIONS

There are three types of employees' associations: voluntary employees' beneficiary associations, supplemental unemployment benefit trusts, and local associations of employees.

Voluntary Employees' Beneficiary Association

A voluntary employees' beneficiary association is an employees' association which provides for the payment of life, sick, accident, or other benefits to its members or their dependents, or designated beneficiaries. Substantially all of the association's operations must be in furtherance of providing those benefits.[42]

The membership of a voluntary employees' beneficiary association must be comprised of individuals who are employees and who have an employment-related common bond such as a common employer, coverage under one or more collective bargaining agreements, or membership in a labor union.[43] An individual is determined to be an "employee" by reference to the legal and bona fide relationship of employer and employee. An employee is an individual who is considered an employee for employment tax purposes or for purposes of a collective bargaining agreement.[44] Additionally, employees on a leave of absence, those working temporarily for other employers or as independent contractors, and those who are retired, disabled, or laid off are considered employees. The surviving spouse and dependents of an employee are also considered employees. It is permissible for as much as 10 percent of the membership to be comprised of nonemployees, so long as they have some employment-related bonds. An example of such an individual would be the proprietor of a business whose employees are members of the association.[45]

Membership in a voluntary employees' beneficiary association must be voluntary. Membership will be considered voluntary if an affirmative act is required on the part of an employee to become a member rather than the designation as a member due to employee status. However, membership is also considered voluntary if employees are required to be members of the association as a condition of their employment and they do not incur a detriment as a result of membership. Membership is also considered voluntary if an employee is required to become a member as a result of a collective bargaining agreement or as an incident of membership in a labor organization.[46]

Benefits that may be paid to members of the association include life, sick, accident, or other benefits.[47] Life benefits are those which are payable by reason of the death of a member or dependent. The benefits may be provided directly to the member or dependent, or through insurance.[48] Sick and accident benefits are those amounts paid to or on behalf of a member or dependent in the event of his illness or personal injury. These benefits may be provided through payment of premiums to a medical benefit or health insurance program or through reimbursement to a member or dependent for amounts expended because of illness or personal injury.[49] "Other benefits" include only benefits which are similar to life, sick, or accident benefits. A benefit is similar if it is intended to safeguard or improve the health of a member or dependent or it protects against a contingency that interrupts or impairs a member's earning power. Such other benefits include, among others, reimbursing vacation expenses, subsidizing recreational activities such as an athletic league, and providing child-care facilities.[50] No part of the association's net earnings may inure to the benefit of any private shareholder or individual, other than in the form of scheduled benefit payments as described above.[51]

Except those organizations which are part of a plan maintained under a collective bargaining agreement, a plan established to provide benefits under a voluntary employees' beneficiary association must meet certain nondiscrimination requirements. The plan meets the nondiscrimination requirements if each class of benefits under the plan is provided under a classification of employees that is set forth in the plan and does not discriminate in favor of highly compensated employees, and if the benefits provided under each class do not discriminate in favor of highly compensated employees. In general, a highly compensated employee is one who, during the current year or the preceding year, owned 5 percent or more of the employer, received more than $50,000 in compensation from the employer, and was among the top 20 percent of employees by compensation, or was an officer of the employer at any time and received more than $45,000 in compensation.

Contributions to a voluntary employees' beneficiary association do not provide the donor with a deduction for a charitable contribution. Application for tax-exempt status may be made by submitting Form 1024 to the IRS.

Supplemental Unemployment Benefit Trusts

A supplemental unemployment benefit trust is tax-exempt under Section 501(c)(17) if it is part of a written plan established and maintained by an employer, his employees, or both, solely for the purpose of providing supplemental unemployment compensation benefits to an employee in the event that the employee is involuntarily separated from service (whether or not such separation is temporary). The separation may result from a reduction in workforce, the discontinuance of a plant or operation, or other similar conditions. Additionally, sickness and accident benefits may be included in the plan if these benefits are subordinate to the unemployment compensation benefits. The plan must provide that no part of the corpus or income of the trust may be used or diverted to any purpose other than to provide such benefits.[52]

The terms of the plan and the payment of benefits must meet the same requirements regarding nondiscrimination as a voluntary employees' beneficiary association.[53] Contributions to a supplemental unemployment benefit trust do not provide the donor with a deduction for a charitable contribution. A supplemental unemployment benefit trust may apply for tax-exempt status by submitting Form 1024 to the IRS. A conformed copy of the plan of which the trust is a part should be submitted with the application.

Local Employees' Associations

A local employees' association is eligible for tax-exempt status under Section 501(c)(4). Such an association is required to limit its membership to employees of a designated person or persons in a particular municipality, and to devote its net earnings exclusively to charitable, educational, or recreational purposes.[54] The association must be of a purely local character. An association is of a purely local character if its business activities are confined to a particular community, place, or district, irrespective of political subdivisions. An association is not purely local in character if its activities are limited only by the borders of a state.[55]

A contribution made to a local association of employees does not provide the donor with a deduction for a charitable contribution. Application for tax-exempt status may be made by submitting Form 1024 to the IRS.

TEACHERS' RETIREMENT FUND ASSOCIATIONS

A teachers' retirement fund association of a purely local character, and organized for the purpose of providing retirement benefits to its members, may qualify for tax-exempt status under Section 501(c)(11). Such an association will so qualify if no part of its net earnings may inure to the benefit of any private shareholder or individual (other than for the payment of retirement benefits), and the income of such association consists solely of amounts received from public taxation, amounts received from assessments on the teaching salaries of members, and income from investments.[56]

Application for tax-exempt status as a teachers' retirement fund association is not made on any specific form. Application may be made by letter to the key district director of the IRS district for the association's main office or place of business. A copy of the association's organizing document should accompany the application letter, and the letter should be signed by an officer of the association.[57]

BENEVOLENT LIFE INSURANCE ASSOCIATIONS, MUTUAL IRRIGATION COMPANIES, COOPERATIVE TELEPHONE COMPANIES, AND LIKE ORGANIZATIONS

The following organizations may apply for tax-exempt status under Section 501(c)(12):

1. Benevolent life insurance associations of a purely local character, and like organizations;
2. Mutual ditch or irrigation companies, and like organizations; and
3. Mutual or cooperative telephone companies, and like organizations.

In order to qualify for tax-exempt status under Section 501(c)(12), at least 85 percent of the organization's income must consist of amounts collected from members for the sole purpose of meeting losses and expenses.[58]

A benevolent life insurance association must be of a purely local character, and its excess funds must be refunded to members or retained in reasonable reserves to meet future losses and expenses. If it issues policies for stipulated cash premiums, or if it requires advance deposits to cover the cost of insurance and maintains investments from which more than 15 percent of its income is derived, it will not be entitled to exemption under Section 501(c)(12). On the other hand, an organization may be entitled to exemption even though it makes advance assessments for the sole purpose of meeting future losses and expenses, provided that the balance of such assessments remaining on hand at the end of the year is retained to meet losses and expenses, or is returned to members.[59] To be "purely local in character" a benevolent life insurance association's activities must be confined to a particular community, place, or district, irrespective of political subdivisions. Activities are not considered to be purely local in character if they are limited only by the borders of a state.[60]

A mutual ditch or irrigation company or a mutual or cooperative telephone company is not required to be purely local in character.

However, these organizations must be organized and operated on a mutual or cooperative basis. In such an association, several persons or organizations unite to provide themselves with a mutually desirable service approximately at cost.[61]

Contributions to organizations exempt under Section 501(c)(12) do not entitle the donor to a deduction for a charitable contribution. Application for tax-exempt status under Section 501(c)(12) is made by submitting Form 1024 to the IRS.

CEMETERY COMPANIES

Cemetery companies may qualify for tax-exempt status under Section 501(c)(13). A nonprofit cemetery company must be owned and operated exclusively for the benefit of its lot owners who hold such lots for bona fide burial purposes and not for the purpose of resale. A mutual cemetery company which also engages in charitable activities, such as the burial of paupers, will be regarded as operating in conformity with this standard. Further, the fact that a mutual cemetery company limits its membership to a particular class of individuals, such as members of a family, will not affect its tax-exempt status, so long as all of the other requirements of Section 501(c)(13) are met.[62]

Any nonprofit corporation, chartered solely for the purpose of the burial or the cremation of bodies, and not permitted by its character to engage in any business not necessarily incident to that purpose, may be exempt from tax under Section 501(c)(13).

No part of the net earnings of a Section 501(c)(13) organization may inure to the benefit of any private shareholder or individual.[63] Earnings of such an organization must be used for the ordinary and necessary expenses of operating, maintaining, and improving the cemetery or crematorium; as payment for the acquisition of cemetery property; and for creating a fund to provide a source of income for the perpetual care of the cemetery or a reasonable reserve for any ordinary or necessary purpose.[64]

Generally, a cemetery company will not qualify for tax-exempt status if it issues preferred stock on or after 28 November 1978.[65] However, a cemetery company may issue common stock and still qualify for tax-exempt status, so long as no dividends may be paid on that common stock.[66] The payment of dividends must be legally prohibited either by the corporation's charter or by applicable state law.[67]

Contributions to exempt cemetery companies, corporations chartered solely for human burial purposes, and perpetual care funds (operated in connection with such exempt organizations) are deductible by the donor as a charitable contribution. However, contributions made for the perpetual care of a particular lot or crypt are not deductible.[68] Application for tax-exempt status as a cemetery company is made by submitting Form 1024 to the IRS.

CREDIT UNIONS

A credit union, organized under state law for mutual purposes, and without profits, may qualify for tax-exempt status under Section 501(c)(14). A credit union may not be organized with capital stock.[69]

There is no specific application form for use in applying for tax-exempt status as a credit union. Any written application may be submitted so long as it indicates the name of the state, the date the credit union was incorporated, that it was formed under state credit union law, and that the state credit union laws with respect to loans, investments, and dividends, if any, are being followed. The following form of statement furnished by the Credit Union National Association is acceptable for application purposes.[70]

Claim for Exemption from Federal Income Tax

The undersigned ______________ (complete name) Credit Union, Inc., ____________________________________ (complete address), including street and number) a credit union operating under the credit union law of the State of __________________ claims exemption from Federal income tax and supplies the following information relative to its operation:

1. Date of incorporation ____________________.
2. It was incorporated under the credit union law of the State of ____________, and is being operated under uniform bylaws adopted by said state.
3. In making loans the state credit union law requirements including their purposes, security and rate of interest charged thereon, are complied with.

4. Its investments are limited to securities which are legal investments for credit unions under the state credit union law.

I, the undersigned, a duly authorized officer of the ______________ Credit Union, Inc., declare that the above information is a true statement of facts concerning the credit union.

Signature of Officer ______________________ Title

MUTUAL INSURANCE COMPANIES

An insurance company may qualify for tax-exempt status under Section 501(c)(15) if it is a mutual company or association (other than life or marine), or if it is a mutual interinsurer or reciprocal underwriter (other than life or marine). In either case, the gross receipts from premiums and gross investment income may not exceed $150,000.[71] Application for tax-exempt status may be made by submitting Form 1024 to the IRS.

CROP FINANCING ORGANIZATIONS

A corporation organized by a farmers' cooperative marketing or purchasing association, or the members thereof, for the purpose of financing the ordinary crop operations of such members or other producers may be tax-exempt under Section 501(c)(16). The marketing or purchasing association which organizes the crop financing organization must itself be tax-exempt as a farmers' cooperative under Section 521, and the crop financing association must be operated in conjunction with the exempt marketing or purchasing association.[72]

There is no specific form to be used in applying for tax-exempt status. Application should be made by letter to the key district director of the IRS district for the organization's main office or place of business.

EMPLOYEE FUNDED PENSION TRUSTS

A trust created prior to 25 June 1959, forming part of a plan to provide for the payment of benefits under a pension plan, was qualified for tax-exempt status under Section 501(c)(18).[73] A funded pension trust was required to be a valid, existing trust under local law, evidenced by an executed written document and funded solely from contributions of employees who are members of the plan.[74] Additionally, the plan (of which the trust was a part) could not discriminate in favor of officers, shareholders, or highly paid employees, and was required to prohibit the diversion of funds for any purpose other than the payment of benefits under the plan.[75]

WAR VETERANS ORGANIZATIONS

A post or organization of past or present members of the Armed Forces of the United States may qualify for tax-exempt status under Section 501(c)(19). In order to qualify, the organization must be organized in the United States or any of its possessions; at least 75 percent of its members must be war veterans, and substantially all of its other members must be individuals who are veterans (but not war veterans) or cadets, or are spouses, widows, or widowers of war veterans, veterans, or cadets; and no part of the net earnings of the organization may inure to the benefit of any private individual or shareholder.[76] "Substantially all" of its members is interpreted to mean 97.5 percent of the total membership. This means that 2.5 percent of an organization's membership may consist of individuals who are not included in one of the veterans groups.

A war veterans organization must be operated exclusively for one or more of the following purposes:[77]

1. To promote the social welfare of the community;
2. To assist disabled and needy war veterans, members of the United States Armed Forces and their dependents, and the widows and orphans of deceased veterans;
3. To provide entertainment, care, and assistance to hospitalized veterans or members of the United States Armed Forces;
4. To carry on programs to perpetuate the memory of deceased veterans and members of the Armed Forces, and to comfort their survivors;
5. To conduct programs for religious, charitable, scientific, literary, or educational purposes;
6. To sponsor or participate in activities of a patriotic nature;
7. To provide insurance benefits for its members or dependents of its members; or
8. To provide social and recreational activities for its members.

An auxiliary unit or society of a veterans organization may also qualify for tax-exempt status under Section 501(c)(19) if: the parent veterans organization is tax-exempt under Section 501(c)(19); the auxiliary is affiliated with, and organized in accordance with, the bylaws and regulations of the parent organization; at least 75 percent of its members are either war veterans or spouses of war veterans, or are related to a war veteran within two degrees of kinship; all of its members are either members of the parent veterans organization, or related to a member of such organization within two degrees of kinship; and no part of its net earnings inure to the benefit of any private shareholder or individual.[78]

A trust or foundation for a war veterans organization may also apply for tax-exempt status provided that: the parent veterans organization is tax-exempt under Section 501(c)(19); the trust or foundation is in existence under local law and, if organized for charitable purposes, has a dissolution provision similar to charitable organizations; the corpus or income cannot be diverted or used other than for the funding of a tax-exempt veterans organization or for religious, charitable, scientific, literary, or educational purposes, or for the prevention of cruelty to children or animals, or for an insurance set-aside; the trust income is not unreasonably accumulated and, if the trust or foundation is not an insurance set-aside, a substantial portion of the income is, in fact, distributed to the parent veterans organization or for the charitable purposes listed above; and the trust or foundation is organized exclusively for one or more of the exempt purposes specifically applicable to the parent organization.[79]

Contributions to a war veterans organization are deductible by the donor as a charitable contribution. Application for tax-exempt status as a war veterans organization is made by submitting Form 1024 to the IRS.

GROUP LEGAL SERVICES PLAN ORGANIZATIONS

For tax years ending prior to 1988, a qualified group legal services plan could have qualified for tax-exempt status under Section 501(c)(20). However, the law that provided for this exemption expired for tax years ending after 1987.[80] A qualified group legal services plan was a separate written plan of an employer established for the exclusive benefit of his or her employees or their spouses or dependents to provide those individuals with personal legal services either through prepayment of, or provision in advance for, legal fees.[81]

BLACK LUNG BENEFIT TRUSTS

A trust established by a person (generally, a coal mine operator) to satisfy his liability for the payment of compensation for disability or death due to pneumoconiosis under federal black lung acts may qualify for tax-exempt status under Section 501(c)(21). There is no particular trust form which must be used; however, the trust must be established and maintained pursuant to a written instrument which definitely and affirmatively prohibits a diversion or use of trust assets not specifically permitted under Section 501(c)(21) or Section 4953(c).[82]

The exclusive purpose of the trust fund set forth under Section 501(c)(21) must be to satisfy, in whole or in part, the liability of the coal mine operator for black lung benefits, to pay premiums for insurance which exclusively covers such liability, and to pay administrative and other incidental expenses of such trust in connection with the operation of the trust and the processing of black lung claims.[83] Section 4953(c) allows amounts of excess contributions to be redistributed to the contributor of those amounts.

No part of the assets of the trust fund may be used for, or diverted to, any purpose other than to support the exclusive purposes of the trust fund as outlined above; to pay into the Black Lung Disability Fund or into the general fund of the United States Treasury; and to make certain permitted investments.[84]

Contributions to a black lung benefit trust are deductible by the donor (generally, the coal mine operator) in accordance with Section 192. However, a 5 percent excise tax is imposed on any amounts contributed to the trust in excess of the deduction limits set forth under Section 192.[85] A 10 percent excise tax is imposed on any expenditures, payments, or investments made which are not specifically permitted under Section 501(c)(21) and Section 4953(c).[86] Finally, an excise tax of 10 percent of the amount involved is imposed on a disqualified person pursuant to any transactions between that person and the trust.[87]

There is no specific form for use in applying for tax-exempt status. A black lung benefit trust should, therefore, apply by letter to the key district director of the IRS for the district for the trust's main office or place of business. A copy of the trust instrument should be included in the application.

WITHDRAWAL LIABILITY PAYMENT FUNDS

A trust, created and organized in the United States pursuant to a written instrument by the plan sponsors of a multiemployer pension plan may be tax-exempt as a withdrawal liability payment fund under Section 501(c)(22) if it is established exclusively to provide funds to meet the liability of employers who withdraw from the multiemployer pension plan. The trust may also pay reasonable and necessary administrative expenses in connection with establishing and operating the trust, and for processing claims against the trust.[88] This type of trust is authorized by Section 4223 of the Employee Retirement Income Security Act of 1974 (ERISA).

A contribution made to the trust fund by the participating employers is deductible for the taxable year in which the contribution is made and which is properly allocable to such taxable year.[89] A contribution which relates to a specified period of time which includes more than one taxable year will be allocated on a pro rata basis to determine the amount of deduction for each taxable year in the period.[90] No deduction is allowed, however, if a contribution does not relate to any specified period.[91]

There is no specific form to use in applying for tax-exempt status. Application may be made by letter to the key district director of the IRS district for the trust's main office or place of business. A copy of the trust instrument should be included in the application.

VETERANS ORGANIZATIONS (CREATED PRIOR TO 1880)

An association organized prior to 1880, in which more than 75 percent of the members are present or past members of the United States Armed Forces, may be exempt under Section 501(c)(23). The principal purpose of the organization must be to provide insurance and other benefits to the veterans or their dependents.[92]

TRUSTS UNDER SECTION 4049 OF THE EMPLOYEE RETIREMENT INCOME SECURITY ACT OF 1974 (ERISA)

A trust under Section 4049 of ERISA is one which is established by the Pension Benefit Guaranty Corporation (PBGC) in connection with a terminated multiemployer pension plan. Such a trust may qualify for tax-exempt status under IRC Section 501(c)(24) if it is used exclusively for receiving liability payments from the persons who were contributing sponsors of the terminated multiemployer pension plan, for making distributions to its participants and beneficiaries, and for defraying the reasonable administrative expenses in connection with the operation of the trust.[93]

RELIGIOUS AND APOSTOLIC ASSOCIATIONS

A religious or apostolic association having a common treasury or community treasury may qualify for tax-exempt status under Section 501(d). A religious or apostolic association may engage in business for the common benefit of its members. However, if such business activity is conducted, the members must include in their gross income their entire pro rata share of the taxable income of the association for the year, whether distributed or not. Any amount included in the members' gross income is treated as a dividend received.[94]

Contributions to a religious or apostolic association do not entitle the donor to a deduction for a charitable contribution. There is no specific form for applying for tax-exempt status. Application must be made by letter to the key district director of the IRS district of the association's main office or place of business.

COOPERATIVE HOSPITAL SERVICE ORGANIZATIONS

A cooperative hospital service organization organized and operated solely to provide certain services, on a centralized basis, to tax-exempt hospitals may qualify for tax-exempt status under Section 501(e). These services include: data processing, purchasing, warehousing, billing and collection, food, clinical, industrial engineering, laboratory, printing, communications, record center, and personnel services.[95] A cooperative hospital service organization must be operated on a cooperative basis, its members being the tax-exempt hospitals for which services are performed. The organization must allocate or pay to its members within 8½ months of the close of its taxable year, all of its net earnings based on the amount of services performed for each of the members.[96] All outstanding capital stock of the organization must be owned by its members.[97]

Contributions to a cooperative hospital service organization are deductible by the donor as a charitable contribution. Application for tax-exempt status is made by submitting Form 1023 to the IRS.

COOPERATIVE SERVICE ORGANIZATIONS OF OPERATING EDUCATIONAL ORGANIZATIONS

Cooperative service organizations organized and controlled by one or more educational organizations may qualify for tax-exempt status under Section 501(f). The cooperative service organization must be organized and operated solely to hold, commingle, and collectively invest and reinvest in stock and securities with funds contributed to the organization by its member educational organizations.[98] The income from such investments, less expenses, must be distributed to the member educational organizations.[99] The member educational organizations must be tax-exempt as educational organizations under Section 501(c)(3) or the income of such organization must be excluded from taxation under Section 115(a).[100]

Contributions to a cooperative service organization entitle the donor to a deduction for a charitable contribution. Application for tax-exempt status is made by submitting Form 1023 to the IRS.

CHILD-CARE ORGANIZATIONS

An organization which provides for the care of children away from their homes may qualify for tax-exempt status under Section 501(k) if the services provided are available to the general public and substantially all of the care provided is for the purpose of enabling individuals to be gainfully employed.

Section 501(k) provides that the term "educational purposes" under Section 501(c)(3) includes such child care organizations; therefore, the actual application for exemption is made under Section 501(c)(3) as an organization devoting substantially all of its activities to "educational purposes."[101]

Contributions to a child-care organization entitle the donor to a deduction for a charitable contribution. Application for tax-exempt status is made by submitting Form 1023 to the IRS.

FARMERS' COOPERATIVES

A farmers' association, organized and operated on a cooperative basis for the purpose of marketing the farm products of the member farmers or for the purpose of purchasing supplies and equipment for the use of its member farmers may qualify for tax-exempt status under Section 521. In order to qualify for such status, a marketing cooperative must return the proceeds of the sale of the products, less necessary operating expenses, to the producers on the basis of either the quantity or the value of the products furnished by each member.[102] Likewise, a purchasing cooperative must turn over purchased supplies and equipment to the member farmers at actual cost, plus necessary expenses.[103]

Application for tax-exempt status as a farmers' cooperative is made by submitting Form 1028 to the IRS.

POLITICAL ORGANIZATIONS

A political organization is a party committee association, fund, or other organization (whether or not incorporated), which is organized and operated for the primary purpose of directly or indirectly accepting contributions or making expenditures, or both, for an exempt function.[104] An exempt function is the activity of influencing or attempting to influence the selection, nomination, election, or appointment of any individual to public office or office in a political organization. Whether an expenditure is for an exempt function depends upon all the facts and circumstances.[105]

A political organization is not taxed on its exempt function income.[106] Exempt function income is any amount received as a contribution of money or other property, membership dues, a membership fee or assessment from a member of the political organization, proceeds from a political fund-raising or entertainment event, proceeds from the sale of political campaign materials which are not received in the ordinary course of any trade or business, or proceeds from conducting certain bingo games to the extent such amount is segregated for use only for the exempt function of the political organization.[107] Other income of a political organization, less certain allowable deductions directly connected with the production of such income, is taxed at the highest corporate rate.[108]

HOMEOWNERS' ASSOCIATIONS

An organization that is a condominium management association or a residential real estate management association may qualify for tax-exempt status under Section 528 as a homeowners' association. Such an organization must be organized and operated to provide for the acquisition, construction, management, maintenance, and care of association property.[109] Substantially all of the homeowners' association's units, lots, or buildings must be used by individuals for residences. For a condominium management association "substantially all" means that at least 85 percent of the total square footage of all units within the project is used by individuals for residences. For a residential real estate management association, "substantially all" means that at least 85 percent of its lots are zoned for residential purposes.[110]

At least 85 percent of a homeowners' association's expenditures for a taxable year must be made for the acquisition, construction, management, maintenance, and care of the association's property. Such expenditures include, among others, expenditures for paying salaries of association employees, paving streets, upkeep of tennis courts, insurance premiums on association property, and replacing common buildings.[111]

A homeowners' association is taxed on all amounts of income except exempt function income. Exempt function income is income derived from owners of residential units or residential lots in their capacity as owner-members, rather than in some other capacity, such as customers for services. At least 60 percent of the association's gross income for the year must consist of exempt function income.[112] No part of the net earnings of a homeowners' association, other than for its exempt purposes, may inure to the benefit of any private shareholder or individual.

In order to be treated as a homeowners' association, an organization must make an election on Form 1120-H. The election must be made for each taxable year and must be made not later than the time, including extensions, for filing an income tax return for the year in which the election is to apply.[113]

CHARITABLE TRUSTS

A charitable trust is one in which all of the unexpired interests are devoted to one or more charitable purposes, and which has provided a charitable contribution deduction for income, estate, or gift tax purposes.[114] If the trust has not been granted tax-exempt status under Section 501(a), the charitable trust is a nonexempt charitable trust, and will be subject to the provisions governing private foundations.[115] In order to avoid treatment as a private foundation, a charitable trust is required to obtain tax-exempt status as a public charity under Section 501(c)(3). The provisions requiring a nonexempt charitable trust to be treated as a private foundation were designed to prevent a donor from establishing a trust for the benefit of charity and making deductible contributions thereto without having to be subject to the requirements and restrictions imposed upon private foundations.

SPLIT INTEREST TRUSTS

A split interest trust is one which has both charitable and noncharitable purposes and which has provided a charitable contribution deduction for income, estate, or gift tax purposes.[116] A split interest trust can be established as a charitable remainder trust in which noncharitable beneficiaries have a lifetime income interest in property with the remainder going to a charitable beneficiary, or as a charitable lead trust in which an income interest in property is granted to a charitable beneficiary with the remainder going to a noncharitable beneficiary. A split interest trust is treated as a private foundation except that it is not subject to the 2 percent excise tax on net investment income under Section 4940 nor to the tax on failure to distribute income under Section 4942. A split interest trust becomes a charitable trust when all of the noncharitable lifetime interests expire.

Charitable Remainder Trusts

There are three types of charitable remainder trusts: a charitable remainder annuity trust, a charitable remainder unitrust, and a pooled income fund.

A charitable remainder annuity trust is a trust which pays, at least annually, a sum certain to one or more noncharitable beneficiaries. The sum certain must be at least 5 percent of the initial net fair market value of all property placed in trust. If an individual is to receive an income interest, the individual must be living at the time the trust is created. In the case of individual beneficiaries, the annuity payments must be made for a term of years not in excess of twenty, or for the lives of the individual beneficiaries.[117] No other amounts may be paid to or for the use of any noncharitable beneficiary.[118] Following the termination of the annual payments, the remainder interest in the trust must be transferred to, or for the use of, a charitable organization.[119] In order to ensure that the sum certain to be distributed is at least 5 percent of the initial fair market value of the property placed in trust, the trust instrument must state that no contributions or bequests other than those used to initially fund the trust may be accepted.[120]

The amount of the charitable contribution deduction provided for the contribution of property to a charitable remainder annuity trust is the fair market value of the remainder interest on the date of the contribution.[121] This amount is calculated by subtracting the actuarial value of the annuity as of the date of the transfer from the net fair market value of the property transferred to the trust.[122] A deduction is not available for the value of the income interest to any beneficiary, whether charitable or noncharitable.[123]

A charitable remainder unitrust is a trust which pays, at least annually, a fixed percentage of the net fair market value of its assets to one or more noncharitable beneficiaries. The fixed percentage may not be less than 5 percent and the assets of the unitrust must be valued at least annually.[124] All other rules relating to charitable remainder annuity trusts apply to charitable remainder unitrusts except that a charitable remainder unitrust may receive additional contributions to the trust after the initial contribution and may provide in its trust instrument that the income beneficiary may be paid the income of the trust in any year that the trust income is less than the required distribution amount.[125] Neither of these options is available to a charitable remainder annuity trust which must provide for sum certain payments.

Both types of charitable remainder trusts are exempt from taxation for any taxable year in which they do not have unrelated business taxable income.[126] For those years in which there is unrelated business taxable income, a charitable remainder trust is subject to regular provisions governing the taxation of trusts.[127]

A pooled income fund is a trust which is maintained by a charitable organization and to which several donors transfer property. Each donor transfers an irrevocable remainder interest in such property to, or for the use of, the charitable organization which maintains the fund. The donor must retain a lifetime income interest in the fund, or grant a lifetime income interest to another noncharitable beneficiary. The property which is transferred by each donor is commingled with property transferred by all other donors to the fund. These funds are then invested and each income interest beneficiary receives income each year. No donor or income beneficiary may be the trustee of the fund, and the fund may receive only those amounts which satisfy all provisions relating to pooled income fund contributions. The pooled income fund may not invest in securities which provide tax-free income (such as state or municipal bonds).[128]

The amount of the charitable contribution deduction which is provided by a transfer of property to a pooled income fund is the value of the remainder interest as of the date of the contribution to the fund. The fund itself is not exempt from taxation as are the charitable remainder annuity trust and the charitable remainder unitrust.

Charitable Lead Trusts

As stated above, a charitable lead trust is one in which an income interest in property is granted to a charitable beneficiary with the remainder going to a noncharitable beneficiary. An income interest must be transferred in the form of a guaranteed annuity lead trust or in the form of a unitrust interest in order for the contribution to be deductible as a charitable contribution.[129] A guaranteed annuity lead trust is designed to pay, at least annually, a determinable amount to a specified charitable beneficiary.[130] A unitrust interest must be set forth in a trust instrument and give a charitable beneficiary the right to receive, at least annually, a fixed percentage of the fair market value of the trust property, such value to be determined annually.[131]

In either case, the donor of the income interest must be treated as the owner of the interest, which means that he is taxed on the annual income of the trust.[132] Distributions to noncharitable beneficiaries may not be made prior to the expiration of all of the charitable income interests; however, a distribution may be made to a noncharitable beneficiary if the amount is paid from a group of assets which have been devoted exclusively to noncharitable purposes by the terms of the trust instrument.[133]

The amount of the charitable contribution deduction provided for the contribution of the property to a charitable lead trust is the fair market value of the income interest on the date of the contribution.[134] This amount is calculated by subtracting the present value of the remainder interest from the fair market value of the transferred property.[135]

Gifts of Less than Donor's Entire Interest

A charitable contribution deduction is not allowed in the case of a contribution of less than the donor's entire interest in contributed property.[136] However, as discussed above, the amount of this type of "split interest" contribution is deductible if the transfer is in trust. There are, however, three exceptions to the prohibition against a charitable deduction for a contribution of less than the donor's entire interest. The exceptions are: (a) a contribution of a remainder interest in a personal residence or farm, (b) a contribution of an undivided portion of the donor's entire interest in the property, and (3) a contribution of property for a qualified conservation purpose.[137]

NOTES

1. IRC Sec. 501(c)(1).
2. Reg. Sec. 1.501(c)(2)-1(a).
3. Reg. Sec. 1.501(c)(2)-1(b).
4. Reg. Sec. 1.501(a).
5. IRC Sec. 501(c)(25)(A).
6. Id.
7. IRC Sec. 501(c)(25)(F).
8. IRC Sec. 501(c)(25)(C).
9. IRC Sec. 501(c)(25)(B).
10. IRC Sec. 501(c)(25)(D).
11. Reg. Sec. 1.501(c)(4)-1(a)(2)(i).
12. Reg. Sec. 1.501(c)(4)-1(a)(1)(i).
13. Reg. Sec. 1.501(c)(4)—1(a)(2)(ii).
14. Id.
15. See Chapter 2 for discussions on Action Organizations.
16. IRC Sec. 170(c). A donation to a Section 501(c)(4) volunteer fire company is deductible if made for exclusively public purposes.
17. Rev. Rul. 71-530, 1971-2 C.B. 237.
18. Reg. Sec. 1.501(c)(5)-1(a)(2).
19. Reg. Sec. 1.501(c)(5)-1(a)(1).
20. Rev. Rul. 75-288, 1975-2 C.B. 212.
21. Reg. Sec. 1.501(c)(6)-1.

22. Id.
23. Id.
24. IRC Sec. 162(e); Reg. Sec. 1.162-20.
25. Reg. Sec. 1.162-15.
26. Reg. Sec. 1.501(c)(7)-1(a).
27. Id.
28. Id.
29. IRC Sec. 501(i).
30. IRS Publication 557 (1988).
31. Reg. Sec. 1.501(c)(7)-1(b).
32. Id.
33. Pub. L. No. 94-568, 10/20/76.
34. Id.
35. IRC Sec. 501(i).
36. IRC Sec. 501(i)(1) and (2).
37. Reg. Sec. 1.501(c)((8)-1(a).
38. Id.
39. Reg. Sec. 1.501(c)(10)-1(a)(1).
40. Reg. Sec. 1.501(c)(10)-1(a)(2).
41. Reg. Sec. 1.501(a)-3.
42. Reg. Sec. 1.501(c)(9)-1(a) and (c).
43. Reg. Sec. 1.501(c)(9)-2(a)(1).
44. Reg. Sec. 1.501(c)(9)-2(b)(1).
45. Reg. Sec. 1.501(c)(9)-2(a).
46. Reg. Sec. 1.501(c)(9)-2(c)(2).
47. Reg. Sec. 1.501(c)(9)-3(a).
48. Reg. Sec. 1.501(c)(9)-3(b).
49. Reg. Sec. 1.501(c)(9)-3(c).
50. Reg. Sec. 1.501(c)(9)-3(d).
51. Reg. Sec. 1.501(c)(9)-4(a).
52. Reg. Sec. 1.501(c)(9)-1(a) and (b).
53. Reg. Sec. 1.501(c)(17)-1(a)(5).
54. Reg. Sec. 1.501(c)(4)-1(b).
55. Reg. Sec. 1.501(c)(12)-1(b).
56. IRC Sec. 501(c)(11).
57. IRS Publication 557 (1988), p. 39.
58. Reg. Sec. 1.501(c)(12)-1(a).
59. Id.
60. Reg. Sec. 1.501(c)(12)-1(b).
61. IRS Publication 557 (1988).
62. Reg. Sec. 1.501(c)(13)-1(a).
63. IRC Sec. 501(c)(13).
64. IRS Publication 557 (1988), p. 35.

65. Reg. Sec. 1.501(c)(13)-(1)(c)(3).
66. IRS Publication 557 (1988), p. 35.
67. Id.
68. Id., p. 36.
69. Reg. Sec. 1.501(c)(14)-1.
70. IRS Publication 557 (1988), p. 36.
71. Reg. Sec. 1.501(c)(15)-1(a)(1).
72. Reg. Sec. 1.501(c)(16)-1.
73. Reg. Sec. 1.501(c)(18)-1(a).
74. Reg. Sec. 1.501(c)(18)-1(b)(1) and (2).
75. IRC Sec. 501(c)(18).
76. Reg. Sec. 1.501(c)(19)-1(a) and (b).
77. Reg. Sec. 1.501(c)(19)-1(c).
78. Reg. Sec. 1.501(c)(19)-1(d).
79. Reg. Sec. 1.501(c)(19)-1(e).
80. IRC Sec. 120(b) and (e); Sec. 501(c)(20).
81. IRC Sec. 120(b).
82. Reg. Sec. 1.501(c)(21)-2.
83. IRC Sec. 501(c)(21)(A).
84. IRC Sec. 501(c)(21)(B).
85. IRC Sec. 4953.
86. IRC Sec. 4952.
87. IRC Sec. 4941 and Sec. 4946.
88. IRC Sec. 501(c)(22)(A).
89. IRC Sec. 194A(a).
90. IRC Sec. 194A(b).
91. IRC Sec. 194A(c).
92. IRC Sec. 501(c)(23).
93. See RIA Federal Tax Coordinator 2d, Sec. D-6114.
94. IRC Sec. 501(d).
95. IRC Sec. 501(e)(1)(A) and (B).
96. IRC Sec. 501(e)(2).
97. IRC Sec. 501(e)(3).
98. IRC Sec. 501(f)(1).
99. Id.
100. IRC Sec. 501(f)(3).
101. IRC Sec. 501(k).
102. Reg. Sec. 1.521-1(a)(1).
103. Reg. Sec. 1.521-1(b).
104. IRC Sec. 527(e)(1).
105. Reg. Sec. 1.527-2(c)(1).
106. IRC Sec. 527(c)(1)(A).
107. IRC Sec. 527(c)(3).

108. IRC Sec. 527(b)(1).
109. Reg. Sec. 1.528-2.
110. Reg. Sec. 1.528-4(a), (b), and (c).
111. Reg. Sec. 1.528-6(a), (b), and (c).
112. Reg. Sec. 1.528-9(a) and IRC Sec. 528(c)(1)(B).
113. Reg. Sec. 1.528-8(a) and (b).
114. IRC Sec. 4947(a).
115. Id. Private foundation provisions will be discussed in Chapter 5.
116. Id.
117. IRC Sec. 664(d)(1)(A).
118. IRC Sec. 664(d)(1)(B).
119. IRC Sec. 664(d)(1)(C).
120. Reg. Sec. 1.664-2(b).
121. Reg. Sec. 1.664-2(c).
122. Id.
123. Reg. Sec. 1.664-2(d).
124. IRC Sec. 664(d)(2).
125. Reg. Sec. 1.664-3(b) and IRC Sec. 664(d)(3).
126. IRC Sec. 664(c).
127. Reg. Sec. 1.664-1(c).
128. IRC Sec. 642(b)(5)(A)-(F).
129. IRC Sec. 170(f)(2)(B).
130. Reg. Sec. 1.170A-6(c)(2)(i).
131. Id.
132. IRC Sec. 170(f)(2)(B) and IRC Sec. 671.
133. Reg. Sec. 1.170A-6(c)(2)(i)(E).
134. Reg. Sec. 1.170A-6(c)(3).
135. Reg.Sec. 1.170A-6(c)(3)(ii).
136. IRC Sec. 170(f)(3)(A).
137. IRC Sec. 170(f)(3)(B).

4

Unrelated Business Taxable Income

In order to maintain its tax-exempt status, an exempt organization must not devote more than an insubstantial part of its activities to carry on activities that are not in furtherance of its exempt purpose. However, in many instances, a tax-exempt organization may carry on a trade or business. A trade or business which is functionally related to the organization's exempt purpose and carried on in furtherance of that purpose poses no threat to the organization's tax-exempt status. A trade or business that is not functionally related to the organization's exempt purpose and not carried on in furtherance of that purpose could jeopardize the organization's tax-exempt status if that trade or business becomes more than an insubstantial part of the organization's activities (i.e., the primary activity).

A middle ground exists between the two extremes of a functionally related trade or business and a nonfunctionally related trade or business which has become the organization's primary activity. This middle ground is a nonfunctionally related trade or business that constitutes only an insubstantial part of the organization's activities, but nonetheless is carried on with a profit motive. In this instance, while the trade or business activity probably would not jeopardize the organization's tax-exempt status because its operation is not the primary purpose of the organization, income generated by the trade or business would not enjoy the tax-free status of the income generated from exempt activities. In fact, such income generated from a nonfunctionally related trade or business is subject to the unrelated business income tax set forth in IRC Sections 511-514.

Traditionally, any income generated by a tax-exempt organization was shielded from taxation. This has caused great concern in the private business sector because in many instances, exempt organizations have been able to use their exempt status to create an unfair competitive advantage over fully taxable organizations conducting the same type of commercial business. For example, it would be possible for an exempt organization to either accumulate larger profits in a shorter period of time than a taxable business, or to expand its business operations more quickly by rolling profits back into the business. This is because a taxable business must use part of its profits to satisfy its tax obligations, whereas an exempt organization is free from such an expenditure.

An exempt organization's commerical ventures may also benefit from the "halo" effect. The halo effect results from the feeling of the general public that a business associated with an exempt organization is somehow "better" than a business conducted by a similar for-profit entity. This means that similar products and services of a charitable organization may be purchased more readily, and therefore, charitable organizations again have the opportunity to compete unfairly with the private business sector.

Congress began to remedy these unfair advantages with the Revenue Act of 1950 by enacting the provisions dealing with feeder organizations and the provisions dealing with unrelated business income. The enactment of such provisions signaled the rejection by Congress of the destination of income test under which, whatever the source of the income, so long as it was used for a tax-exempt purpose, it was not taxable.

Since 1950, tax-exempt organizations which allow nonfunctionally related business activities to become the primary purpose of the organization lose their tax-exempt status via the feeder organization provisions. If such business activities become a substantial part of the organization's activities, but do not become the primary purpose of the organization, income generated by those business activities is taxed under the unrelated business income provisions. Caution is appropriate in conducting business activities because, as previously discussed, there is no definition set forth regarding "substantial" or "primary." This means that an organization's business activity, and the amount thereof in relation to its other activities, will be judged based on the facts and circumstances present. Additionally, if an organization wants to avoid taxation altogether, it must make certain that it engages solely in functionally related business activities.

When originally enacted in 1950, the unrelated business income provisions did not cover churches, governmental organizations, social welfare organizations, social clubs, fraternal benefit societies, employee benefit societies, veteran societies, credit unions, certain life insurance companies, or cemeteries. These exclusions from the unrelated business income rules created inequities in treatment among the various types of exempt organizations. Therefore, under the Tax Reform Act of 1969, Congress made the previously excluded organizations subject to the unrelated business income provisions. Currently, only governmental instrumentalities exempt from tax under Section 501(c)(1) and 501(a), are excluded from the unrelated business income provisions.[1] The provisions do apply, however, to any college or university which is an agency or instrumentality of a government or of any political subdivision thereof, or which is owned or operated by a government or any political subdivision thereof.[2] The term "government" includes any foreign government (to the extent not contrary to a treaty) and all domestic governments.[3]

DEFINITION OF UNRELATED TRADE OR BUSINESS INCOME

Section 512 defines unrelated business taxable income as gross income derived from any unrelated trade or business regularly carried on less the deductions for business expenses directly connected with carrying on the trade or business. An unrelated trade or business is one which is not substantially related to the exempt purpose of the organization (aside from the need for income or funds or the use made of profits derived therefrom).[4] Thus, the determination of whether an organization will be taxed on business income requires the examination of three questions: is the activity from which the income is derived a trade or business; is the trade or business regularly carried on; and is the trade or business substantially related to the organization's exempt purposes?

Trade or Business

The unrelated business income tax was adopted primarily to combat what was perceived as an unfair competitive advantage of tax-exempt organizations over nonexempt business endeavors with which they compete.[5] Therefore, the overriding consideration in determining that a trade or business exists is whether the business activity is conducted in a competitive or commercial manner. More specifically, to be considered a trade or business for purposes of the unrelated business income tax, an activity must possess the characteristics of a trade or business within the meaning of Section 162.[6] That is, the activity must be carried on for the production of income from the sale of goods or performance of services.[7] It is not significant that the activity does not actually result in profits, nor is it significant that profits cannot reasonably be expected.[8] It is significant only that the activity is conducted with the intention to produce income, as in a commercial venture.

It is clear that the facts and circumstances of each case will be of utmost importance in determining whether the activity in question is a trade or business. In this regard, it should be noted that an activity from which an organization derives gross income will not lose identity as a trade or business merely because it is carried on within a larger aggregate of similar activities or within a larger complex of other endeavors which may or may not be related to the organization's exempt purpose.[9] For example, a hospital pharmacy by the regular sale of pharmaceutical supplies to the general public does not lose its identity as a trade or business even though the pharmacy also furnishes supplies to the hospital and to patients of the hospital in keeping with its exempt purpose.[10] Soliciting, selling, and publishing commercial advertisements for publication as an exempt organization's periodical which contains editorial matter related to the organization's exempt purpose is a second example of a trade or business being carried on within a larger complex of activities.[11]

Regularly Carried On

Income from a trade or business is subject to unrelated business income tax only if the trade or business is regularly carried on. To determine whether a trade or business is regularly carried on, consideration must be given to the frequency and continuity with which the income-producing activities are conducted and the manner in which they are pursued.[12] Applying the requirement in light of the purpose of the unrelated business income tax, which is to place exempt organization business activities on the same tax basis as nonexempt business endeavors, specific business activities of an exempt organization will be deemed to be "regularly carried on" if they manifest a frequency and a continuity and are pursued in a manner generally similar to comparable commercial activities of nonexempt organizations.[13]

The normal time span of activities is considered when comparing income-producing activities of a tax-exempt organization to those conducted by a nonexempt organization. An activity conducted by a tax-exempt organization for only a few weeks would not be considered regularly carried on if similar commercial ventures were conducted on a year-round basis by nonexempt organizations.[14] For example, the operation of a sandwich stand by a hospital auxiliary for only two weeks at a state fair would not constitute the regular conduct of a trade or business because similar activities conducted by a nonexempt food establishment would be conducted on a year-round basis.[15] However, the conduct of year-round business activities for one day each week would constitute the regular carrying on of a trade or business.[16] For example, the operation of a commercial parking lot every Saturday, year-round, would be the regular conduct of a trade or business.[17]

The seasonal nature of an activity is also considered in determining if it is regularly carried on. If an activity is normally conducted on a seasonal basis by nonexempt commercial organizations, and the same activity is conducted during a significant portion of the season by an exempt organization, such actions would constitute the regular conduct of a trade or business. For example, operating a horse-racing track for several weeks of a year would be considered the regular conduct of a trade or business because it is customary to conduct horse racing only during a particular season.[18]

Intermittently conducted business activities must be compared with the manner in which similar commercial activities are normally pursued by nonexempt organizations in order to determine if the activity is regularly carried on. Generally, business activities conducted by an exempt organization will not be considered regularly carried on if the activities are engaged in only discontinuously or periodically and are not conducted with the competitive and promotional efforts typical of commercial endeavors.[19] For example, the publication of advertising in programs for sports events or for music or drama performances will not ordinarily be deemed to be the regular conducting of a trade or business.[20] Similarly, if an exempt organization sells goods or services to a particular class of persons in pursuance of its exempt purpose, casual sales to the general public will not be treated as regular sales. For example, casual sales made to the general public by a college bookstore maintained primarily for the convenience of its students, or the casual sale of pharmaceutical supplies to the general public by a hospital pharmacy maintained primarily for the convenience of its patients, will not be considered regular sales.[21] However, if such nonqualifying sales are not merely casual, but are systematically and consistently promoted and carried on, they will be considered regular sales.[22]

Income-producing or fund-raising activities lasting only a short period of time will not ordinarily be treated as regularly carried on if they recur only occasionally or sporadically.[23] Furthermore, the fact that such activities are conducted on an annually recurrent basis will not cause them to be regarded as regularly carried on. For example, income derived from an annual fund-raising dinner for charity would not be income from a regularly carried on trade or business.[24]

Substantially Unrelated

An unrelated trade or business is one in which the conduct of the trade or business is not substantially related (other than through the production of funds) to the exempt purposes of the organization.[25] The determination of whether the activities are substantially related to the organization's exempt purpose necessitates an examination of the relationship between the business activities which generate the income and the accomplishment of the organization's exempt purposes.[26] The trade or business is related to the exempt purpose only where the conduct of the business activities has a "substantial causal relationship" to the achievement of the organization's exempt purpose.[27] According to the Regulations, this requires an examination of the facts and circumstances to determine if the production or distribution of the goods, or the performance of the services from which the income is derived, "contributes importantly" to the accomplishment of those purposes.[28] The size and extent of the activities involved in relation to the nature and extent of the exempt function which they purport to serve are the factors which should be considered in determining whether the activities contribute importantly to the accomplishment of the organization's exempt purpose.[29] If an organization conducts an activity that is, in part, related to the performance of its exempt function, but conducts the activity on a larger scale than is reasonably necessary for performance of such exempt function, the gross income attributable to that portion of the activity in excess of the needs of the exempt function would be income from the conduct of an unrelated trade or business, because that excess activity would not contribute importantly to the accomplishment of the exempt purpose of the organization.[30]

Several cases and revenue rulings illustrate the concept of a "substantially related" trade or business and also unrelated activities which give rise to the unrelated business income tax.

Example 1. An exempt university alumni association, organized for the promotion of education by assisting the university, financially and otherwise, and by encouraging its member alumni to do the same, also operates a travel tour program for its members and their families. There is no formal educational program associated with the tours and they do not differ from regular commercially operated tours. The organization is engaged in an unrelated business because there is no causal relationship between the travel tour activity and the achievement of the association's exempt purpose, and because the activity does not contribute importantly to the accomplishment of the association's exempt purpose.[31]

Example 2. An exempt hospital operates a parking lot with use limited to staff, patients, and visitors. The operation of the parking lot is substantially related to the hospital's exempt purpose and does not constitute an unrelated trade or business. The same conclusion would be reached if the hospital operated a gift shop or cafeteria with use of such facilities restricted to the same classes of persons.[32]

Example 3. An exempt hospital operates a pharmacy which sells drugs and pharmaceutical supplies to its patients. Such activity would not be considered an unrelated trade or business. However, if the pharmacy also sold drugs and pharmaceutical supplies to private patients of physicians (even those physicians with offices in the hospital-owned medical building), such activity would be considered an unrelated trade or business to the extent of such sales.[33] A different result was reached in the case of a rural hospital which allowed sales to patients of private physicians. In this case the activity was related to the hospital's exempt purpose (promotion of health) because the existence of the pharmacy was instrumental in attracting and maintaining a medical staff for the community hospital.[34]

Example 4. An exempt museum operates a dining room, a cafeteria, and a snack bar for use by the museum staff, employees, and members of the public visiting the museum. These activities do not constitute an unrelated trade or business because the operation of such facilities contributes importantly to the accomplishment of the museum's educational purpose by enabling visitors to spend a greater amount of their time viewing the exhibits than would be the case if they had to seek outside restaurants at mealtime. Also, such facilities make it possible for museum staff and employees to remain in the museum throughout the day. However, to the extent that the general public uses such facilities, the museum would be subject to unrelated business income tax on the income produced therefrom.[35]

Example 5. An art museum exempt as an educational organization operates a gift shop in which it sells greeting cards with printed reproductions of artwork on display in the museum. The museum also publishes a catalog in which it solicits mail orders for the greeting cards. The catalog is available at a small charge and is advertised in magazines and other publications throughout the year. In addition, the gift shop sells the cards at quantity discounts to retail stores. As a result, a large number of cards are sold at a significant profit. Notwithstanding the fact that the cards are promoted and sold in a commercial manner at a profit, and in competition with commercial greeting card publishers, the activity is substantially related to the museum's exempt purpose. This is because the sale of the greeting cards contributes importantly to the achievement of the museum's educational purpose by enhancing public awareness, interest, and appreciation of art, and encourages people to visit the museum to share in its educational programs.[36]

Assume that the same gift shop also sells scientific books and souvenir items of the city in which the museum is located. In this instance, the sale of each particular line of merchandise would be considered separately to determine if it is related to the exempt purpose. Neither the scientific books nor the souvenir items have any causal relationship to art or artistic endeavor and, therefore, the sale of these items does not contribute importantly to the accomplishment of the organization's exempt educational purpose. Under different circumstances, the sale of the scientific items could be held related to the exempt educational purpose of some other exempt educational organization, but that fact does not alter the conclusion in this situation.

Additionally, the museum, by the sale of the scientific books and souvenir items, does not lose its identity as a trade or business merely because the museum also sells articles which do contribute importantly to the accomplishment of its exempt purpose. Therefore, the sale of those articles constitutes an unrelated trade or business.[37]

Example 6. An exempt senior citizens center operates a beauty parlor and barber shop. Such activities were found to be substantially related to the organization's exempt purpose because of the convenience provided to the senior citizens.[38] On the other hand, the sale of appliances to the senior citizens was found not substantially related to the center's exempt purpose.[39]

INCOME FROM PERFORMANCE OF EXEMPT FUNCTIONS

Gross income derived from charges for the performance of exempt functions does not constitute gross income from the conduct of an unrelated trade or business.[40] For example, a tax-exempt organization operates a school for training children in the performing arts such as acting, singing, and dancing. An essential part of the students' training is their participation in performances before an audience. Gross income is derived from admission charges. Because the income realized from the performances derives from activities which contribute importantly to the accomplishment of the organization's exempt purpose, it does not constitute gross income from an unrelated trade or business.[41]

The fact that unrelated trade or business income is not derived from charges for the performance of exempt functions can be further illustrated by a second example. An exempt trade union presents a trade show in which members of its industry join in an exhibition of industry products. The trade association derives income from charges made to exhibitors for exhibit space and also derives income from admission fees charged to patrons or viewers of the show. The purpose of the show is to promote and stimulate interest in, and demand for, the industry's products in general. The show is conducted in a manner reasonably calculated to achieve that purpose. The show does not operate as a sales facility for individual exhibitors. Because the stimulation of demand for the industry's product in general is one of the purposes for which exemption is granted, and because promoting, organizing, and conducting the exhibition contribute importantly to the achievement of the trade association's exempt purpose, such activities do not constitute an unrelated trade or business. Therefore, income from those activities would not be unrelated trade or business income.[42]

DISPOSITION OF PRODUCTS OF EXEMPT FUNCTIONS

Gross income that results from the sale of products which result from the performance of the exempt functions of an exempt organization does not constitute unrelated trade or business income. This is so, however, only if the product is sold in substantially the same state that it was upon the completion of the exempt function.[43] For example, if an exempt charitable organization engages in a program of rehabilitation of handicapped persons, income from the sale of articles made by such persons as a part of their rehabilitation training would not be gross income from the conduct of an unrelated trade or business.[44] Such income would be from the sale of products, the production of which contributed importantly to the accomplishment of the organization's exempt purposes.[45]

On the other hand, if a product is further processed beyond its state upon completion of the exempt functions, the gross income derived therefrom would be from the conduct of an unrelated trade or business. Thus, if an exempt scientific organization maintains an experimental dairy herd, income from the sale of milk and cream produced in the ordinary course of operation of the project would not be gross income from the conduct of an unrelated trade or business. However, if the milk and cream are further manufactured into food items such as ice cream or cheese, the gross income from the sale of such products would be from the conduct of an unrelated trade or business unless the additional manufacturing activities themselves contribute importantly to the accomplishment of an exempt purpose of the organization.[46]

DUAL USE OF ASSETS OR FACILITIES

An asset or facility used by an exempt organization in the conduct of its exempt function may also be used by the organization in a commercial endeavor. In such cases, income from the commercial endeavor would be income from an unrelated trade or business. The mere fact that the asset or facility is used for exempt functions does not, by itself, make the income from the commercial endeavor gross income from a related trade or business.[47] The test to determine whether the income in question is from a related trade or business is whether the activities which produced the income contribute importantly to the accomplishment of the organization's exempt purposes.[48] For example, an exempt museum operates a theater auditorium continuously during the hours the museum is open to the public. The theater is a principal feature of the museum and was specially designed and equipped for showing educational films in connection with the museum's program of public education in the arts and sciences. During the evening hours when the museum is closed, the museum operates the theater as an ordinary motion picture theater for public entertainment. Gross income derived from the operation of the theater would constitute unrelated business income. Gross income derived from the operation of the theater to show educational films to museum visitors would not be unrelated business income.[49]

EXPLOITATION OF EXEMPT FUNCTIONS

Some activities conducted by an exempt organization in the pursuit of its exempt functions may generate intangibles, such as good will, which are capable of being exploited in a commercial endeavor. In such cases, unless the commercial endeavor itself contributes importantly to the accomplishment of an exempt purpose, the income generated thereform is gross income from the conduct of an unrelated trade or business. The mere fact that the income which results from the commercial endeavor depends, in part, upon an exempt function of the organization does not make it gross income from a related trade or business.[50] The following examples illustrate the exploitation of exempt functions.

Example 1. An exempt scientific organization has built an excellent reputation in the field of biological research. It exploits its reputation by regularly selling endorsements of various items of laboratory equipment to manufacturers. The endorsement activity does not contribute importantly to the accomplishment of the organization's exempt purpose. Therefore, the income derived from the endorsement activity is gross income from an unrelated trade or business.[51]

Example 2. During the school year, an exempt university sponsors the appearance of professional theater companies and symphony orchestras which present drama and musical performances for the students and faculty members. Members of the general public are also admitted. The university advertises the performances and supervises advance ticket sales at university facilities. The university derives income from the conduct of the performances. Such income does not constitute unrelated trade or business income because, although the presentation of the performances exploits the intangible generated by the university's exempt functions—the presence of the student body and faculty—such presentations contribute importantly to the overall educational and cultural function of the university.[52]

Example 3. An exempt business league enters into an arrangement with an advertising agency and regularly mails brochures, pamphlets, and other commercial advertising materials to its members. The business league charges the agency an agreed amount per enclosure. The distribution of the advertising materials does not contribute importantly to the accomplishment of the business league's exempt purpose. Therefore, the payments made by the advertising agency constitute gross income from an unrelated trade or business.[53]

Income from the sale of advertising is, perhaps, the most prevalent example of income from the exploitation of an exempt function. For example, an exempt organization formed to promote the advancement of public interest in classical music owns a radio station and operates it in a manner which contributes importantly to the accomplishment of its exempt purposes. However, in the course of its operation, the organization derives gross income from the regular sale of advertising time and services to commercial advertisers in the manner of an ordinary commercial station. Neither the sale of such time nor the performance of such services contributes importantly to the accomplishment of the organization's exempt purposes; therefore, such income is gross income from an unrelated trade or business.[54] Generally, income realized by an exempt organization from the sale of advertising in a periodical which it publishes is gross income from an unrelated trade or business activity involving the exploitation of an exempt activity, namely, the circulation and readership of the periodical developed through the production and distribution of the readership content of the periodical.[55]

In the instances where the advertising activity is found to exploit the exempt activity of the circulation and readership of the periodical, the unrelated business taxable income attributable to the sale of advertising must be calculated. Four rules are applicable in making this calculation:

1. If the direct advertising costs of an exempt organization's periodical exceed gross advertising income, the excess is allowable as a deduction in determining unrelated business taxable income from any

unrelated trade or business activity carried on by the organization.[56] Direct advertising costs are all items of deduction which are directly connected with the sale and publication of the advertising.[57] Gross advertising income is the total amount derived from the unrelated advertising activities.[58]

2. If the gross advertising income of an exempt organization's periodical exceeds direct advertising costs, items of deduction attributable to the production and distribution of the readership content of the periodical will qualify as deductions directly connected with the unrelated advertising taxable income to the extent that these deductions exceed circulation income and do not result in a loss. These expenses, however, are not taken into account in computing the unrelated business taxable income of any unrelated trade or business activity other than the advertising activity.[59]
3. If the periodical's circulation income equals or exceeds its readership costs, the unrelated business taxable income attributable to the periodical is the excess of the gross advertising income over the direct advertising costs.[60]
4. If the periodical's readership costs exceed its circulation income, the unrelated business taxable income is the excess of the total income attributable to the periodical over the total periodical costs.[61] The total income attributable to the periodical is the sum of its gross advertising income and its circulation income.[62] The total periodical costs are the total deductions attributable to the periodical, including direct advertising costs, and total readership costs.[63]

Circulation income is income attributable to the production, distribution, or circulation of a periodical, including amounts realized from the sale or distribution of the readership content of the periodical.[64] When the right to receive an exempt organization periodical is associated with membership or similar status in the organization for which dues, fees, or other charges are received, circulation income includes the portion of such membership receipts which are allocable to the periodical. Allocable membership receipts are the amounts which would have been charged and paid for the periodical if it were that of a taxable organization, published for profit, and the member was an unrelated party dealing with the taxable organization at arm's length.[65]

Allocable membership receipts for a periodical are determined in accordance with the following rules:[66]

(a) If at least 20 percent of the total circulation of a periodical consists of sales to nonmembers, the subscription price of the periodical to such nonmembers will determine the price of the periodical.

(b) If less than 20 percent of the total circulation of the periodical is from sales to nonmembers and the membership dues from at least 20 percent of the members who do not receive the periodical are less than the membership dues received from the members who do receive the periodical, the difference between the two amounts determines the price of the periodical.

(c) If neither of the conditions described in (1) or (2) applies, the amount of the membership receipts allocated to the periodical equals the organization's membership receipts multiplied by a fraction, the numerator of which is the total periodical costs, and the denominator of which is these costs plus the cost of the organization's other exempt activities.

These rules may be illustrated by the following examples:[67]

Example 1. U is an exempt scientific organization with 10,000 members, each of whom pays annual dues of $15. One of U's activities is the publication of a monthly periodical which is distributed to all its members. U also distributes 5,000 additional copies of its periodical to nonmember subscribers at a cost of $10 per year. Because the nonmember circulation of U's periodical represents 33.3 percent of its total circulation, the subscription price charged to nonmembers will be used to determine the portion of U's membership receipts allocable to the periodical. Thus, U's allocable membership receipts will be $100,000 ($10 times 10,000 members), and U's total circulation income for the periodical will be $150,000 ($100,000 from members plus $50,000 from sales to nonmembers).

Example 2. Assume the facts as stated in Example (1), except that U sells only 500 copies of its periodical to nonmembers, at a price of $10 per year. Assume further that U's members may elect not to receive the periodical, in which case their dues are reduced from $15 per year to $6 per year, and that only 3,000 members elect to receive the periodical and pay the full dues of $15 per year. U's stated subscription price of $9 to members consistently results in an excess of total income (including gross advertising income) attributable to the periodical over total costs of the periodical. Because the 500 copies of the periodical distributed to nonmembers represent only 14 percent of the 3,500 copies distributed, the $10 subscription price charged to nonmembers will not be used in determining the portion of membership receipts allocable to the periodical. On the other hand, since 70 percent of the members elect not to receive the periodical and pay $9 less per year in dues, such $9 price will be used in determining the subscription price charged to members. Thus, the allocable membership receipts will be $9 per member, or $27,000 ($9 times 3,000 copies) and U's total circulation income will be $32,000 ($27,000 from members plus $5,000 from nonmembers).

Example 3. (a) W, an exempt trade association, has 800 members each of whom pays annual dues of $50. W publishes a monthly journal, the editorial content and advertising of which are directed to the business interests of its own members. The journal is distributed to all of W's members and no receipts are derived from nonmembers.

(b) W has total receipts of $100,000 of which $40,000 ($50 times 800) are membership receipts and $60,000 is gross advertising income. W's total costs for the journal and other exempt activities are $100,000. W has total periodical costs of $76,000 of which $41,000 are direct advertising costs and $35,000 are readership costs.

In this instance, no copies of the periodical are available to nonmembers. Therefore, an allocation of the membership receipts must be made. Based upon pro rata allocation of membership receipts ($40,000) by a fraction, the numerator of which is total periodical costs ($76,000) and the denominator of which is the total costs of the journal and the other exempt activities ($100,000), $30,400 ($76,000/$100,000 times $40,000) of membership receipts is circulation income.

Readership costs include expenses, depreciation, or similar items that are directly connected with the production and distribution of the readership content of the periodical, and which otherwise would be allowable as a deduction in determining unrelated business taxable income if the production and distribution constituted an unrelated trade or business activity.[68]

The rules set forth in numbers 1 through 4 earlier may be illustrated by the following examples.[69]

Example 1. X, an exempt trade association, publishes a single periodical which carries advertising. During 1971, X realizes a total of $40,000 from the sale of advertising in the periodical (gross advertising income) and $60,000 from sales of the periodical to members and nonmembers (circulation income). The total periodical costs are $90,000 of which $50,000 is directly connected with the sale and publication of advertising (direct advertising costs) and $40,000 is attributable to the production and distribution of the readership content (readership costs). Because the direct advertising costs of the periodical ($50,000) exceed gross advertising income ($40,000), the unrelated business taxable income attributable to advertising is determined solely on the basis of the income and deductions directly connected with the production and sale of the advertising:

Gross advertising revenue	$ 40,000
Direct advertising costs	(50,000)
Loss attributable to advertising	$(10,000)

X has realized a loss of $10,000 from its advertising activity. This loss is an allowable deduction in computing X's unrelated business taxable income derived from any other unrelated trade or business activity.

Example 2. Assume the facts as stated in Example 1, except that the circulation income of X's periodical is $100,000 instead of $60,000 and that of the total periodical costs, $25,000 are direct advertising costs, and $65,000 are readership costs. Since the circulation income ($100,000) exceeds the total readership costs ($65,000), the unrelated business taxable income attributable to the advertising activity is $15,000, the excess of gross advertising income ($40,000) over direct advertising costs ($25,000).

Example 3. Assume the facts as stated in Example 1, except that of the total periodical costs, $20,000 are direct advertising costs and $70,000 are readership costs. Since the readership costs of the periodical ($70,000) exceed the circulation income ($60,000), the unrelated business taxable income attributable to advertising is the excess of the total income attributable to the periodical over the total periodical costs. Thus, X has unrelated business taxable income attributable to the advertising activity of $10,000 ($100,000 total income attributable to the periodical less $90,000 total periodical costs).

Example 4. Assume the facts as stated in Example 1, except that the total periodical costs are $120,000 of which $30,000 are direct advertising costs and $90,000 are readership costs. Since the readership costs of the periodical ($90,000) exceed the circulation income ($60,000), the unrelated business taxable income attributable to advertising is the excess, if any, of the total income attributable to the periodical over the total periodical costs. Since the total income of the periodical ($100,000) does not exceed the total periodical costs ($120,000), X has not derived any unrelated business taxable income from the advertising activity. Further, only $70,000 of the $90,000 of readership costs may be deducted in computing unrelated business taxable income since such costs may be deducted, to the extent they exceed circulation income, only to the extent they do not result in a loss from the advertising activity. Thus, there is no loss from such activity, and no amount may be deducted on this account in computing X's unrelated trade or business income derived from any other unrelated trade or business activity.

If an organization which is subject to unrelated business income tax publishes two or more periodicals for the production of income, it may treat the gross income from all (but not less than all) of the periodicals and the items of deduction directly connected with such periodicals on a consolidated basis, as if such periodicals were one periodical for purposes of determining the amount of unrelated business taxable income derived from the sale of advertising in the periodicals. The organization must follow this procedure on a consistent basis, and once adopted, it is binding, unless the organization obtains consent from the IRS for a change in reporting procedures.[70]

An organization publishes a periodical for the production of income if the periodical generates gross advertising income equal to at least 25 percent of the readership costs of the periodical, and an examination of the facts and circumstances indicates that the publication of the periodical is an activity engaged in for profit. A profit motive may exist even if there are no actual profits in a particular year.[71]

However, if the sale of advertising contributes importantly to an organization's exempt purposes, income derived therefrom will not be unrelated business taxable income. For example, an exempt university provides facilities, instruction, and faculty supervision for a campus newspaper operated by its students. In addition to news items and additional commentary, the newspaper publishes paid advertising which is solicited, sold, and published by the students, under the supervision of the university. Because the advertising activities are conducted by the students as part of their education program, the income therefrom is not unrelated trade or business income.[72]

EXCLUDED ACTIVITIES

Several activities are specifically excluded from the term "unrelated trade or business." These activities include:

1. Any trade or business in which substantially all the work in carrying on such trade or business is performed for the organization without compensation (volunteer).[73] For example, an exempt orphanage operating a retail store and selling to the general public would not have income from an unrelated trade or business if substantially all of the work is performed by volunteers.[74]
2. Any trade or business carried on by a 501(c)(3) organization or by a 511(a)(2)(B) governmental college or university, primarily for the convenience of its members, students, patients, officers, or employees. For example, a laundry operated by a college for the use of laundering dormitory linens and student's clothing would not be an unrelated trade or business. Excluded for a local association of employees described in Section 501(c)(4) (and organized before 27 May 1969), is the selling of items of work-related clothes and equipment and items normally sold through vending machines, food dispensing facilities, or by snack bars for the convenience of its members at their usual place of employment.[75]
3. Any trade or business which consists of selling merchandise, substantially all of which has been received by the organization as gifts or contributions.[76] For example, thrift shops operated by an exempt organization where those desiring to benefit such organization contribute old clothes, books, furniture, and other articles to be sold to the general public with the proceeds going to the organization would not be an unrelated trade or business.
4. Certain bingo games are not considered an unrelated trade or business. A bingo game would qualify for this exclusion only if it is legal and not in violation of either state or local law. Additionally, the games must not be conducted in a jurisdiction in which such games are ordinarily conducted on a commercial basis. The wagers must be placed, the winners determined, and prizes or other property distributed in the presence of all persons placing wagers in that game.[77]
5. Certain services, including data processing, purchasing, warehousing, billing and collection, clinical, industrial engineering, laboratory, printing, and personnel provided by one hospital to certain other hospitals will not be unrelated trade or business.[78] this is the case so long as each recipient hospital of each specific service is an exempt or a governmental hospital which services fewer than 100 inpatients, the services performed are related to the recipient hospital's exempt function, and the services are provided at cost.[79]

For example, a large metropolitan hospital provides various services to other hospitals. The hospital furnishes a purchasing service to hospitals N and O, a data-processing service to hospitals R and S, and a food service to hospitals X and Y. All of the hospitals serve fewer than 100 inpatients except hospital N. The services are furnished at cost to all hospitals except that hospital R is charged a fee in excess of cost for its use of the data-processing service. The purchasing service constitutes an unrelated trade or business because it is not provided solely to hospitals serving fewer than 100 inpatients. The data-processing service constitutes an unrelated trade or business because it is provided at a fee in excess of cost. The food service is not an unrelated trade or business because it satisfies the three requirements enumerated above.[80]

6. Qualified public entertainment activities do not constitute an unrelated trade or business. A public entertainment activity, which is considered to be a related trade or business for Section 51(c)(3), (4), or (5) organizations, is one that is traditionally conducted at a fair or exposition promoting agriculture and education, including any activity whose purpose is designed to attract the public to fairs or expositions or to promote the breeding of animals or the development of products or equipment. A qualified public entertainment activity is one which is conducted by a qualifying organization in conjunction with an international, national, regional, or local fair or exposition; in accordance with state law that permits the activity to be operated or conducted solely by such an organization or by an agency, instrumentality, or political subdivision of the state; or in accordance with state law that permits an organization to be granted a license to conduct activity for not more than twenty days on paying the state a lower percentage of the revenue from the activity than the state charges nonqualifying organizations that conduct similar activities. A qualifying organization is an organization described in Section 501(c)(3), (4), or (5) that regularly conducts an agricultural and educational fair or exposition as one of its substantial exempt purposes.[81]
7. Qualified convention or trade show activities conducted at a convention, annual meeting, or trade show will not constitute an unrelated trade or business. A qualified convention or trade show activity is one which is traditionally carried on by a qualifying organization in conjunction with an international, national, state, regional, or local convention, annual meeting, or show if one of the purposes of the organization in sponsoring the activity is promoting and stimulating interest in, and demand for, the products

and services of that industry, or educating the attendees regarding new developments or products and services related to the exempt activities of the organization, and if the show is designed to achieve its purpose through the character of the exhibits and the extent of the industry products that are displayed. A qualifying organization is one described in Section 501(c)(3), (4), (5) and (6) which regularly conducts, as one of its substantial exempt purposes, a show that stimulates interest in, and demand for, the products of a particular industry, or that educates the attendees regarding new developments or products and services related to the exempt activities of the organization.[82]

The rental of display space to exhibitors (including exhibitors who are suppliers) at a qualified convention or trade show will not be considered an unrelated trade or business even if the exhibitors who rent the space are permitted to sell or solicit orders. For this purpose, a supplier's exhibit is one in which the exhibitor displays goods or services that are supplied to, rather than by, members of the qualifying organization in the conduct of these members' own trades or businesses.[83]

8. The exchange or rental of an exempt organization's mailing list to another exempt organization will not constitute an unrelated trade or business.[84]
9. Activities relating to the distribution of low-cost articles incidental to soliciting charitable contributions do not constitute an unrelated trade or business. A distribution is considered incidental to the solicitation of a charitable contribution if the recipient did not request the distribution, the distribution is made without the express consent of the recipient, and the article is accompanied by a request for a charitable contribution to the organization and a statement that the recipient may keep the low cost article regardless of whether a contribution is made. An article is considered low cost if the aggregate cost of an item or items distributed to a single recipient is not more than $5, to be adjusted annually for any cost of living increases.[85]

MODIFICATIONS TO UNRELATED TRADE OR BUSINESS INCOME

The statute and regulations set forth several items of modification in the calculation of unrelated taxable business income. Whether a particular item of income falls within any of the modifications is a question of the facts and circumstances in each specific case.[86] The modifications are as follows.

Dividends, Interest, Annuities, and Royalties

Generally, income from investments is not taxed as unrelated business income. Therefore, income from dividends, interest, annuities, and royalties is not included in unrelated business income.[87] (Certain exceptions to these modifications apply in connection with debt-financed property and controlled corporations.)[88] These items of investment income are excluded from unrelated business income because such income is passive-type income and does not place the exempt organization in a commercial activity in competition with a taxable business. In other words, it is not income of the type that is derived from an exempt organization's "unfair" competitive advantage.

Securities Loans

Subject to certain requirements, income realized as a result of payments received with respect to securities loans will constitute investment income and not unrelated business income.[89] To be treated as investment income, the securities must be loaned under an agreement between the parties which provides reasonable procedures to implement the obligation of the borrower to furnish collateral to the exempt organization lender, such collateral to have a fair market value on each business day that the loan is outstanding in an amount not less than the fair market value of the security at the close of business on the preceding business day. The agreement must also permit the exempt-organization lender to terminate the loan upon notice of not more than five business days, and must provide that securities identical to the transferred securities will be returned to the exempt organization lender upon the termination of the loan.[90]

Gains and Losses from the Disposition of Property

Gains or losses from the sale, exchange, or other disposition of property will not be included in the computation of unrelated business taxable income. This exclusion does not apply to the gain derived from the sale or other disposition of debt-financed property, to stock in trade or other property which would properly be included in inventory if on hand at the close of the tax year, to property held primarily for sale to customers in the ordinary course of a trade or business, or to the cutting of timber which an organization has elected to consider as a sale or exchange of the timber.[91]

Lapse or Termination of Options

Gain derived from the lapse or termination of options which were written in connection with the exempt organization's investment activities will not constitute unrelated business income. The exclusion will not apply if the securities upon which the options are written are held by the organization as inventory or for sale to customers in the ordinary course of a trade or business or if the organization is engaged in the trade or business of writing options.[92]

Research

Income derived from research activities by a tax-exempt organization is excluded from unrelated business income. However, the exclusion is limited by the type of organization and the type of research. Income derived by any type of exempt organization from research for the United States, any of its agencies or instrumentalities, or a state or political subdivision thereof, and all deductions directly connected with such income are excluded in computing unrelated business taxable income. An organization operated primarily to carry on fundamental research, the results of which are freely available to the general public, may exclude all income and all directly connected deductions therefrom in computing its unrelated business taxable income. A college, university, or hospital, however, may exclude all income and deductions derived from research activities whether that research is fundamental or applied.[93]

Net Operating Losses

The net operating loss, as provided for in Section 172, is allowed in computing unrelated business taxable income. However, the net operating loss carryback or carryover is determined without regard to any amount of income or deduction that has been specifically excluded in computing unrelated business taxable income. For example, a loss from an unrelated trade or business will not be diminished because royalty income was received.[94] The effect of including such income or deductions would be to tax-exempt income because unrelated business losses would be offset by income from excluded items such as dividends, interest, and royalties. This offset would reduce the loss that could be applied against unrelated business profits of prior or future tax years.[95]

Prior taxable years for which an organization was not subject to unrelated business income tax are not taken into account in computing the current net operating loss. Thus, the net operating loss is not a carryback to such preceding taxable year, and the net operating loss carryover to succeeding taxable years is not reduced by the related income of those prior years.[96]

A net operating loss carryback or carryover is allowed only from a tax year for which the organization is subject to the unrelated business income tax.[97] However, in determining the span of years for which a net operating loss may be carried back or forward for purposes of computing the net operating loss, taxable years in which the organization was not subject to the unrelated business income tax, are taken into account.[98] For example, if an organization is subject to the unrelated business income tax provisions in 1990 and has a net operating loss for that year, the last taxable year to which any part of that loss may be carried over is the year 2005, regardless of whether the organization is subject to the unrelated business income tax in any of the intervening years.

Charitable Contributions Deduction

An exempt organization taxable at corporate rates is entitled to a deduction for charitable contributions of up to 10 percent of the organization's unrelated business taxable income computed without regard to the deduction for contributions.[99] In the case of a trust, the contribution is limited to the extent set out in Section 170 for income tax purposes, except that the limitation must be calculated with reference to the unrelated business taxable income without regard to the deduction for contributions (in lieu of *with* regard to adjusted gross income as per Section 170).[100]

Specific Deduction

A specific deduction is allowed in computing unrelated business taxable income in an amount which is the lesser of $1,000 or the gross income derived from any unrelated trade or business.[101] An organization is entitled to only one such deduction regardless of how many unrelated businesses it operates. However, in the case of a diocese, province of a religious order, or a convention or association of churches, each of their local units is entitled to a separate deduction provided that the unit does not file a separate return.[102] The deduction is not allowable in computing the net operating loss or the net operating loss deduction.

Services Provided Under Federal License

Income from a trade or business carried on by a religious order or by an educational organization maintained by the order will not be considered income from an unrelated trade or business. This is the case so long as the trade or business consists of providing services under a license issued by a federal regulatory agency, has been operated by the organization since prior to 27 May 1959, uses less than 10 percent of the net income each year for purposes other than that for which the exemption was granted, and establishes to the satisfaction of the IRS that the rates charged for the services are competitive with rates charged for such services by taxable entities.[103]

Rental Income

Rental income, which is considered passive income, is excluded from unrelated business taxable income. However, this exclusion may be limited depending upon the type of property that is rented. Generally, income from the rental of real property is excluded from unrelated business taxable income for taxable years beginning after 31 December 1969.[104] Income from the rental of personal property is generally taxed, but will be excluded from unrelated business taxable income if such property is leased with real property and the rental income attributable to the personal property is an incidental amount of the total rental income received.[105] Rental income attributable to personal property is considered an incidental amount of the total rental income if such income does not exceed 10 percent of the total rental income from all the property leased.[106] This determination is made when the personal property is first placed in service by the lessee.[107] For example, if the rental income attributable to the personal property leased is determined to be $2,000 per year, and the total rental income from all property leased is $10,000 per year, the $2,000 amount is included in unrelated business taxable income because it is in excess of 10 percent of the total rental income from all property leased.

Property is placed in service by the lessee when it is first subject to the lessee's use in accordance with the terms of the lease.[108] For example, property subject to a lease entered into on 14 December 1990, for a term commencing on 1 January 1991, will be considered as placed in service as of 1 January 1991, regardless of when the property is actually used for the first time by the lessee.

All rental income, including that derived from the rental of real property, will be included in unrelated business taxable income if more than 50 percent of the total rental income received is attributable to personal property, such amount to be determined at the time the personal property is first placed in service by the lessee.[109] Likewise, all rental income will be included in unrelated business taxable income if the amount of such rental income is dependent, in whole or in part, on the income or profits derived from the leased property, other than an amount based on a fixed percentage of the gross receipts or sales.[110]

If rental income from the rental of personal property exceeds 10 percent, but does not exceed 50 percent of that rental income, only that portion of rental income attributable to the rental of personal property is included in unrelated business taxable income. The rule regarding rental income can be summarized as follows:

Percentage of Rental Income from Personal Property	**Amount of Rental Income Included in UBTI**
10% or less	None
Greater than 10% up to 50%	All income attributable to personal property rental
Greater than 50%	All rental income

The use of multiple leases for properties which have an integrated use (one or more leases for real property and another lease or leases for personal property to be used upon such real property), will not avoid the classification of the appropriate rental income as unrelated business taxable income. In such cases, all leases covering properties with an integrated use are considered to be one lease.[111] Additionally, regardless of the terms set forth in any lease, rental income will be allocated between the real property and the personal property according to the amount of rental income "actually attributable" to such property.[112] For example, on 1 January 1990, an exempt organization executes two leases with lessee. One lease is for the rental of a computer with a stated annual rental of $1,000. The other lease is for the rental of office space in which to use the computer, with a stated annual rental of $9,000. The total annual rent due under both leases for 1990 is $10,000. Although the organization executed separate leases, they will be treated as one lease because the property covered thereunder has an "integrated use." Under these terms no part of the rental income would be included in the exempt organization's unrelated business taxable income because only an incidental amount (10%) of the total rental income is from the rental of personal property.

However, at the time the computer was first placed in service, 1 January 1990, and taking both leases into consideration, it is determined that, notwithstanding the terms of the leases, $3,000, or 30 percent of the rent is actually attributable to the computer. Because the amount of rental income attributable to the personal property, 30 percent, is more than an incidental amount, the entire amount so attributable, $3,000, must be included in the organization's unrelated business taxable income.

The amount of rental income attributable to the office space, $7,000, may be excluded from the organization's unrelated business taxable income because rental income attributable to the personal property (the computer) is not greater than 50 percent. If the rental income attributable to the computer had been determined to be $6,000, the entire amount of rental income, $10,000, would be included because the amount attributable to the personal property would be greater than 50 percent.

If additional or substitute personal property is placed in service which thereby increases the rent attributable to the personal property by 100 percent or more, or if there is a modification of the lease by which there is a change in the rent charged (whether or not there is a change in the amount of personal property rented), the rent attributable to personal property must be recomputed to determine what portion of rental income, if any, is excludable from unrelated business taxable income. Any change in the treatment of rents as a result of a recomputation is effective only for the period beginning with the event that triggered the recomputation.[113] For example, suppose an exempt organization executes two leases with a lessee each for a term beginning 1 January 1990. One is for the lease of a computer with a stated annual rental of $4,000. The other is for the rental of office space in which to use the computer, at a stated annual rental of $6,000. The leases have an "integrated" use, and so, must be considered together. As such, the total annual rental is $10,000. On the day that the personal property is placed in service, it is determined that the rent has been appropriately apportioned between the two leases. Therefore, only the $4,000 attributable to the computer lease is included in unrelated business taxable income.

Assume that the terms of the leases allow a yearly increase or decrease in rent depending upon the prevailing market value at the beginning of each new yearly lease term. On 1 January 1991, the annual rent attributable to the computer is increased to $6,000, and the annual rent on the office space is decreased to $4,000. The rental income from the real property continues to be excluded from unrelated business taxable income. This is true notwithstanding the fact that the rental income attributable to the personal property is now greater than 50 percent of the total rental income. Here, there was neither an increase in rental income caused by adding or substituting personal property, nor a modification of the lease which changed the amount of rent charged. Remember that the terms of the leases provided for the increase or decrease in rent; the terms of the leases were not modified to do so.

Assume now that two additional computers are placed in service on 1 January 1992, and that additional office space is rented. The rent on the computers is increased to $8,000 per year, and the rent on the office space is increased to $7,000 per year. Because personal property has been added and the rent attributable to the personal property increased by at least 100 percent as a result, a redetermination must be made. Now, the total annual rental income is $15,000. The rental income attributable to the personal property is now 53.3 percent ($8,000/ $15,000); therefore, all rental income, from both personal property and real property, is included in unrelated business taxable income.

Suppose that on 10 July 1992, the leases are modified to set the rent on the computers at $2,000 each, regardless of market value. The rent on the office space remains at $7,000. Because there has been a modification of the terms of the lease, a redetermination must be made as of 10 July 1992, the date of the modification. On that date, the total annual rental income is $13,000, $2,000 for each of the three computers, and $7,000 for the office space. Notwithstanding the terms of the leases, it is determined that, as of the modification date, only $1,000 of the annual rental income is attributable to the computers and the remaining $12,000 is attributable to the office space. Because the rental income attributable to the personal property is less than 10 percent ($1,000/ $13,000), none of the rental income is included in unrelated business taxable income. This change becomes effective as of the modification date, 10 July 1992.

Payments for the use or occupancy of real property such as hotel rooms or boarding houses will not be excluded from unrelated business taxable income if services are also provided to the occupant. Generally, services are considered as being rendered to the occupant if they are primariy for the convenience of the occupant and are other than those usually or customarily rendered in connection with the rental of rooms or other space for occupancy only. Such services include maid service in hotels. However, the furnishing of heat and light, the cleaning of public areas, and the collection of trash would not be considered as services rendered to the occupant.[114]

INCOME FROM CONTROLLED ORGANIZATIONS

Generally, interest, annuities, royalties, and rents are excluded from unrelated business taxable income because of their passive nature. However, a certain portion of such income is included in the unrelated business taxable income of an exempt organization which receives such income from another organization which it controls. This rule applies even if the activity from which the exempt controlling organization derives such income does not represent a regularly carried on trade or business.[115] An exempt organization controls a stock corporation if it holds at least 80 percent of the total combined voting power of all classes of stock entitled to vote and at least 80 percent of the total number of shares of all other classes of stock in the corporation.[116] An organization controls a nonstock organization if at least 80 percent of the directors or trustees of such organization are either representatives of or directly or indirectly controlled by the organization. A trustee or director is a representative of an exempt organization if he or she is a trustee, director, agent, or employee of the exempt organization. A trustee or director is controlled by an exempt organization if such organization has the power to remove such trustee or director and designate a new trustee or director.[117]

If control of an organization is acquired or relinquished during the taxable year, only those amounts of interest, annuities, royalties, and rents attributable to that portion of the year in which the organization had control will be included in its unrelated business taxable income.[118] Amounts included in unrelated business taxable income under any other provision are not also included in unrelated business taxable income from a controlled organization.[119] However, if a controlling organization derives rental income from the lease of debt-financed property to a controlled organization, the amount of unrelated business taxable income therefrom is first calculated under the provisions relating to income from controlled organizations. If any part of the income escapes taxation under those provisions, that part of the income then becomes subject to the debt-financed property provisions.[120]

The amount of unrelated business taxable income attributable to a controlling organization depends, in part, on whether the controlled organization is an exempt organization or a nonexempt organization. The actual amount is calculated by applying a specific ratio to the total income derived from the controlled organization. The controlling organization is also entitled to all deductions directly connected with the income which must be included.[121]

If the controlled organization is also an exempt organization, the unrelated business taxable income that the controlling organization must recognize is that amount of income which bears the same ratio to interest, annuities, royalties, and rents received from the controlled organization as the unrelated business taxable income of the controlled organization bears to the taxable income of the controlled organization, computed as though the controlled organization were not exempt. If the controlled organization's taxable income determined for this purpose is less than its unrelated business taxable income, the entire amount of income received by the controlling organization from the controlled organization, and the entire amount of deductions directly connected to that income, must be included in the controlling organization's unrelated business taxable income.[122]

This is illustrated by the following example. A, an exempt organization, owns all of the stock of B, another exempt organization. During the year, A rents a laboratory to B for $30,000 per year. A's total deductions for the year with respect to the leased property are $15,000 per year. If B were not an exempt organization, its total taxable income would be $600,000, disregarding rent paid to A. B's unrelated business taxable income is $200,000, disregarding rent paid to A. Under these circumstances, $5,000 of the rent paid by B will be included by A as net rental income in determining its unrelated business taxable income, computed as follows:

B's unrelated business taxable income (disregarding rent paid to A)	$200,000
B's taxable income (computed as though B were not an exempt organization and disregarding rent paid to A)	600,000
Ratio ($200,000/$600,000)	1/3
Total rent paid to A	30,000
Total deductions attributable to leased property	15,000
Rental income treated as gross income from an unrelated trade or business (⅓ of $30,000)	10,000
Less deductions directly connected with such income (⅓ of $15,000)	5,000
Net rental income included by A in computing its unrelated business taxable income	$ 5,000

If the taxable income of the controlled organization is equal to or less than the organization's unrelated business taxable income, the entire amount of income received from the controlled organization, and all deductions directly connected to that income, would be included by the controlling organization in computing its unrelated business taxable income. For example, if B's taxable income, in this example, was $100,000, which is less than its unrelated business taxable income of $200,000, the total rent ($30,000) and the total deductions directly connected to that rent ($15,000) would be included by A in computing its unrelated business taxable income.

If the controlled organization is not exempt from taxation, the unrelated business taxable income that must be recognized by the controlling organization is that amount of income which bears the same ratio to interest, annuities, royalties, and rents received by the controlling organization from the controlled organization as the "excess taxable income" of the controlled organization bears to the greater of the taxable income of the controlled organization or the excess taxable income of the controlled organization. Both of these amounts are determined without regard to any amount paid directly or indirectly to the controlling organization.[123] Excess taxable income is defined as the excess of the controlled organization's taxable income over the amount of such taxable income which, if derived directly by the controlling organization, would not be unrelated business taxable income.[124]

This is illustrated by the following example. A, an exempt university, owns all of the stock of M, a nonexempt organization. During the year, A leases a factory and a dormitory to M for a total annual rental of $100,000. During the year, disregarding the rent paid to A, M has $500,000 of taxable income, $150,000 from a dormitory for students of A university, and $350,000 from the operation of a factory which is not related to A's exempt purpose. A's deductions for the year with regard to the leased property are $4,000 for the dormitory and $16,000 for the factory. Under these circumstances, $56,000 of the rent paid by M will be included by A as net rental income in determining its unrelated business taxable income, computed as follows:[125]

M's unrelated business taxable income (disregarding rent paid to A)	$500,000
Less taxable income from dormitory (amounts that would not be unrelated business taxable income if received by A, the controlling organization)	150,000
Excess taxable income	$350,000

Ratio ($350,000/$500,000)	7/10
Total rent paid to A	$100,000
Total deductions ($4,000 + $16,000)	20,000
Rental income treated as gross income from an unrelated trade or business (7/10 of $100,000)	70,000
Less deductions directly connected with such income (7/10 of $20,000)	14,000
Net rental income included by A in computing its unrelated business taxable income	$ 56,000

If the excess taxable income of the controlled organization is equal to or less than the organization's unrelated business taxable income, the entire amount of income received from the controlled organization, and all deductions directly connected to that income, would be included by the controlling organization in computing its unrelated business taxable income. For example, suppose that M's taxable income (disregarding rent paid to A) is $300,000, consisting of $350,000 from the operation of the factory and a $50,000 loss from the operation of the dormitory. M's excess taxable income would be $300,000 because none of M's income would be unrelated business taxable income if received directly by A. The ratio of M's excess taxable income to its taxable income is, therefore, one ($300,000/$300,000). Thus, all the rent received by A from M ($100,000), and all the deductions directly connected therewith ($20,000), are included by A in computing its unrelated business taxable income.[126]

UNRELATED DEBT-FINANCED PROPERTY

The Tax Reform Act of 1969 amended Section 514 to provide that income from unrelated debt-financed property would be taxable to the exempt corporation in the same proportion as the amount of debt on the property. Prior to that time, it was possible for an exempt organization to use its status to purchase property using debt financing and then using the tax-exempt income generated by that property to repay the debt. This placed the exempt organization at an unfair advantage over taxable organizations.

"Unrelated debt-financed income" with respect to each debt-financed property is calculated by multiplying the total income derived from, or on account of such property, by the "debt/basis" percentage. The debt/basis percentage is the "average acquisition indebtedness" attributable to the debt-financed property divided by the "average adjusted basis" of such property.[127] This calculation is illustrated by the following example. An exempt organization owns an office building which produced $100,000 of gross rental income. The average adjusted basis of the building for the year is $200,000, and the average acquisition indebtedness is $50,000. The debt/basis percentage for the year is 25 percent ($50,000/$200,000). Thus, the unrelated debt-financed income from the property is $25,000 (25% of $100,000).

Debt-financed property is any property which is held to produce income and with respect to which there is an acquisition indebtedness at any time during the taxable year. This includes income produced from rental real estate, tangible personal property, and corporate stock if such property is subject to acquisition indebtedness at any time during the taxable year.[128] The term "income" is not limited to recurring income, but also applies to gains from the disposition of property if there was an acquisition indebtedness outstanding with respect to such property at any time during the twelve-month period preceding the date of disposition.[129] In the case of a sale of debt-financed property, the amount included in income is calculated by mulitplying the gain by a percentage obtained by dividing the highest acquisition indebtedness of the property during the twelve months preceding the sale by the average adjusted basis of the property.[130]

There are several exceptions to the definition of debt-financed property. To the extent that the use of any property is substantially related to the organization's exempt function (aside from the organization's need for income or the use it makes of the profits derived), it will not be treated as debt-financed property.[131] If substantially all of the property is used for a substantially related function, no part of the property will be considered to be debt financed.

At least 85 percent or more of the property must be devoted to the organization's exempt purpose in order to meet the "substantially all" standard.[132] If less than substantially all of the property is used for a purpose other than one which is substantially related to the organization's exempt purpose, only that portion of the property used for an exempt purpose will not be treated as debt-financed property. The extent to which the property is used for the organization's exempt purpose is determined by examining all of the facts and circumstances, including a comparison of the amount of time that the property is used for exempt purposes with total time the property is used, and/or a comparison of the portion of the property that is used for exempt purposes with the portion of the property that is used for all purposes.[133]

These comparisons are illustrated by the following examples:

Example 1. A, an exempt organization owns a piece of office equipment which it purchased with borrowed funds. A uses the equipment in the performance of its exempt purpose more than 90 percent of the time that the equipment is in service. The other 10 percent of the time, A leases the equipment to B, a corporation. Because A uses the equipment for exempt purposes at least 85 percent of the time that the equipment is in service, the ''substantially all'' test is met and no portion of the equipment is treated as debt-financed property.

Example 2. L, an exempt organization owns a ten-story office building which it purchased with borrowed funds. During the year, seven stories of the building were used by L to conduct its exempt facilities. L leased the remaining three stories to K, a corporation, for $20,000 per year. Expenses of $6,000 were associated with the building, $5,000 allocable to the seven stories used by L, and $1,000 allocable to the three stories used by K. Because less than 85 percent of the building is used for exempt purposes, an allocable portion of the income from the lease of the three stories must be included by L in calculating its unrelated business taxable income. To determine such amount it is necessary to calculate the debt/basis percentage for the year. Assume that the average adjusted basis of the building for the year is $200,000 and that the average acquisition indebtedness was $80,000. The debt/basis percentage is determined by dividing the allocable part of the average acquisition indebtedness by the allocable part of the average adjusted basis of the property. The allocable part of the average acquisition indebtedness is $24,000 (3/10 of $80,000), and the allocable part of the average adjusted basis is $60,000 (3/10 of $200,000). Thus, the debt/basis percentage is 40 percent ($24,000/$60,000) of the expense attributable to the leased portion of the building in its calculation of unrelated business taxable income for the year. The actual amount of net rental income that L must include is $7,600, calculated as follows:

Total rental income	$20,000
Deductions directly connected with rental income	1,000
Debit/basis percentage ($24,000/$60,000)	40%

Rental income treated as gross income from an unrelated trade or business (40% of $20,000)	8,000
Less allowable portion of deductions directly connected with such income (40% of $1,000)	400
Net rental included by L in computing its unrelated business taxable income from unrelated debt-financed property	$ 7,600

Example 3. Assume the same facts as in Example 2, except that on 31 December L sells the building and realizes a gain of $10,000, and that the highest acquisition indebtedness on the property was $80,000 throughout the year. The allocable portion of the gain is subject to tax. The amount of tax is determined by multiplying the gain related to the nonexempt use, $3,000 (3/10 of $10,000), by the ratio which the allocable part of the highest acquisition indebtedness for the twelve-month period preceding the date of sale, $24,000 (3/10 of $80,000), is of the allocable part of the average adjusted basis, $60,000 (3/10 of $200,000). Thus, the debt/basis percentage with respect to computing the gain (or loss) derived from the sale of the building is 40 percent ($24,000/ $60,000). Consequently, $1,200 (40 percent of $3,000) of the gain from the sale of the building must be included by L in calculating its unrelated business taxable income.

Acquisition Indebtedness

With respect to any debt-financed property, the acquisition indebtedness is the amount of principal indebtedness incurred by an exempt organization in acquiring or improving the property. Acquisition indebtedness also includes any indebtedness incurred prior to the acquisition or improvement of the property, but only if the indebtedness would not have been incurred "but for" the acquisition or improvement of the property. If the indebtedness is incurred after the acquisition or improvement of the property, acquisition indebtedness exists only if the indebtedness would not have been incurred but for the acquisition or improvement, and if the incurrence of the indebtedness was reasonably foreseeable at the time of the acquisition or improvement.[134]

Average acquisition indebtedness is calculated by adding the amount of the outstanding principal indebtedness on the first day of each calendar month during the taxable year that the organization holds the property, and then dividing this sum by the total number of months during the taxable year that the organization held the property. A fractional part of a month is treated as a full month for purposes of the calculation.[135] The calculation is illustrated by the following example.[136] On 10 July 1990, X, an exempt educational organization, purchases an office building for $510,000 using $300,000 of borrowed funds. Beginning on 20 July 1990, the organization makes payments of $21,000 per month ($20,000 of principal and $1,000 of interest). The average acquisition indebtedness for 1990 is $250,000, calculated as follows:

Month	**Indebtedness on the first day of each calendar month that the property is held**
July	$ 300,000
August	280,000
September	260,000
October	240,000
November	220,000
December	200,000
Total	$1,500,000
Average acquisition indebtedness ($1,500,000/6 months)	$ 250,000

When calculating the average acquisition indebtedness, it is important to remember that consideration is given to each calendar month in which the property is held, not just each calendar month for which there is indebtedness. For example, assume that an exempt organization purchases property on 12 January 1990, with an outstanding principal indebtedness of $300,000 on that date. Beginning on 20 January 1990, the organization makes payments of $50,000 per month so that the debt is retired within six months. The average acquisition indebtedness for 1990 is $87,500, calculated as follows:

Month	**Indebtedness on the first day of each calendar month that the property is held**
January	$ 300,000
February	250,000

March	200,000
April	150,000
May	100,000
June	50,000
July through December	—
Total	$1,050,000
Average acquisition indebtedness ($1,050,000/12 months)	$ 87,500

If property is acquired (or improvements made) for an indeterminate price, the initial acquisition indebtedness is the fair market value of the property (or improvement) on the date of acquisition (or the date of completion of the improvement) less any down payment or other initial payment applied to the principal indebtedness.[137] For example, if an exempt organization acquires an office building for a down payment of $200,000, and an agreement to pay 20 percent of the income generated by the building for twenty years, neither the sales price nor the amount which the organization is obligated to pay in the future is certain. Therefore, the initial acquisition indebtedness is the fair market value of the building on the date of acquisition less the down payment. Assuming that the fair market value of the property on the date of acquisition was $600,000, the initial acquisition indebtedness would be $400,000 ($600,000 minus $200,000).

Property used for exempt purposes is not considered debt-financed property; therefore, indebtedness with respect to such property is not acquisition indebtedness. However, if an organization converts such property to a nonexempt use which results in the property being treated as debt financed, the outstanding principal indebtedness with respect to the property will thereafter be treated as acquisition indebtedness. For example, assume that a university borrowed funds in 1986 and acquired an apartment building as housing for married students and used the building as such until 1990 when it rented the building to the public for nonexempt purposes. The outstanding principal indebtedness becomes acquisition indebtedness as of 1990, the time when the building is first rented to the public.[138]

If an organization sells property that would have been subject to acquisition indebtedness except that the property was used for an exempt purpose, and acquires debt-financed property without retiring the indebtedness on the first property, the retained debt becomes acquisition indebtedness with respect to the newly acquired property. For example, to house its administrative offices, an exempt organization purchased a building with $600,000 of its own funds and $400,000 of borrowed funds secured by a pledge of its securities. It later sold the building for $1,000,000, but did not redeem the pledge. The organization then used the proceeds to acquire an apartment building which it rented to the public for nonexempt purposes. The debt of $400,000 became acquisition indebtedness with respect to the apartment even though the office building was not debt-financed property.[139]

If property is acquired subject to a mortgage, the amount of the outstanding principal indebtedness secured by the mortgage is treated as acquisition indebtedness even though the organization does not assume or agree to pay the indebtedness.[140] A lien which is similar to a mortgage, such as a deed of trust, is treated in the same manner as a mortgage.[141]

These rules are applicable to property acquired by purchase, bequest, devise, or gift. However, if property is acquired by bequest or devise, the outstanding principal debt secured by the mortgage is not treated as acquisition indebtedness for the ten-year period following the date of acquisition.[142] If property subject to a mortgage is acquired by gift, the outstanding principal debt secured by the mortgage is not treated as acquisition indebtedness during the ten-year period following the date of the gift, so long as the mortgage was placed on the property more than five years prior to the date of the gift, and the property was held by the donor for more than five years prior to the date of the gift.[143]

The exceptions relating to property received by bequest, devise, or gift do not apply if an organization assumes and agrees to pay all, or any part of, indebtedness secured by the mortgage or makes any payment for the equity owned by the decedent or the donor of the property.[144]

The extension, renewal, or refinancing of an existing debt are considered as a continuation of that debt to the extent that the outstanding principal amount of the existing debt does not increase. If the principal amount of the modified obligation exceeds the outstanding principal amount of the existing debt, the excess is treated as a separate debt for purposes of the debt-financed property provisions.[145]

Average Adjusted Basis

The average adjusted basis of debt-financed property is the average amount of the adjusted basis of such property during that part of the taxable year that it is held by the organization. It is the average of the adjusted basis of the property as of the first day during the taxable year that the organization holds the property and the adjusted basis of the property as of the last day during the taxable year that the organization holds the property.[146] Adjustments (such as depreciation adjustments) must be made for the entire period that the organization has held the property regardless of whether the organization was exempt during prior taxable years.[147]

The amount of the average adjusted basis is calculated as follows. On 26 August 1990, X, an exempt hospital, purchased an office building for $200,000 using $150,000 of borrowed funds. During 1990, $10,000 of depreciation was the only adjustment to basis. As of 31 December 1990, the adjusted basis of the building was $190,000 ($200,000 minus $10,000). The average adjusted basis of the property would be $195,000 ($200,000 plus $190,000 divided by 2).

PROPERTY NOT TREATED AS DEBT-FINANCED PROPERTY

To the extent that the gross income from any property is treated as income from the conduct of an unrelated trade or business, such property will not be treated as debt-financed property.[148] Also, property that generates income which is otherwise included in the computation of unrelated business taxable income will not be treated as debt-financed property. This would include rents from personal property otherwise includable, and rents and interest from controlled organizations which are otherwise includable.[149] This is illustrated by the following example.[150] Z, an exempt university, owns all of the stock of M, a nonexempt corporation. During the year, Z leases a factory to M. The factory is unrelated to Z's exempt purpose. Z also leases to M a dormitory for the students of Z for a total annual rent of $100,000, $80,000 for the factory and $20,000 for the dormitory. During the year, M has $500,000 of taxable income, disregarding the rent paid to Z, $150,000 from the dormitory and $350,000 from the factory. The factory is subject to a mortgage of $150,000. Its average adjusted basis for the year is $300,000. Z's deductions for the year with respect to the leased property are $4,000 for the dormitory and $16,000 for the factory. Only that portion of the rental income that is excluded from the computation of unrelated business taxable income, as income from the rental of real property and not included in such computation after application of the provisions regarding rental income received from a controlled organization, will be subject to the provisions regarding debt-financed income.

Because all of the rental income received by Z is derived from real property, all such income would be excluded from the computation of Z's unrelated business taxable income. However, 70 percent of the rent paid to Z with respect to the factory and 70 percent of the deductions directly connected with such rent must be taken into account by Z in determining its unrelated business taxable income, pursuant to the provisions regarding income received from a controlled organization. This amount is computed as follows:

M's taxable income (disregarding rent paid to Z)	$500,000
Less taxable income from dormitory	150,000
Excess taxable income	350,000
Ratio ($350,000/$500,000)	7/10
Total rent paid to Z	100,000
Total deductions ($4,000 + $16,000)	20,000
Rental income treated as gross income from an unrelated trade or business (7/10 of $100,000)	70,000
Less deductions directly connected with such income (7/10 of $20,000)	14,000
Net rental income included by Z in computing its unrelated business taxable income	$ 56,000

Because only that portion of the rent derived from the factory, and the deductions directly connected with such rent not taken into account as income and deductions derived from a controlled organization, may be included in computing unrelated business taxable income under the debt-financed property provisions, only $10,000 ($80,000 minus $70,000) of rent and $2,000 ($16,000 minus $14,000) of deductions are so taken into account. The portion of such amounts to be included in the calculation of unrelated trade or business income is determined by multiplying the $10,000 of income and $2,000 of deductions by the debt/basis percentage. The debt/basis percentage is the ratio which the average acquisition indebtedness ($150,000) is of the average adjusted basis of the property ($300,000). Thus, the debt/basis percentage for the year is 50 percent ($150,000/$300,000). Under these circumstances, Z must include net rental income of $4,000 in its unrelated business taxable income for the year, computed as follows:

Total rents	$10,000
Deductions directly connected with such rents	2,000
Debt/basis percentage ($150,000/$300,000)	50%
Rental income treated as gross income from an unrelated trade or business (50% of $10,000)	5,000
Less allowable portion of deductions directly connected with such income (50% of $2,000)	1,000
Net rental income included by Z in computing its unrelated business taxable income from debt-financed rental property	$ 4,000

The total amount that Z must include in its calculation of unrelated business taxable income pursuant to the rental income derived from M with regard to the factory is $60,000 ($56,000 because the income was derived from a controlled organization, and $4,000 because the income was derived from debt-financed property).

Property which is used for certain research activities is not considered debt-financed property.[151] Property which is used in a trade or business that is related to the organization's exempt function such as a trade or business carried on for the convenience of certain exempt organizations, or a trade or business which sells only donated items, will not be considered debt-financed property.[152]

Neighborhood Land Rule

Property which meets the requirements of the neighborhood land rule will not be considered debt-financed property.[153] The neighborhood land rule provides that if an exempt organization acquires real property for the principal purpose of using it in performance of its exempt purpose within ten years of the time of acquisition, the property will not be treated as debt-financed property provided that (1) the property is in the neighborhood of other property owned by the organization and used in the performance of its exempt purpose, and (2) the organization does not abandon its intent to use the land to perform its exempt purpose within the ten-year period.[154]

The acquired property is considered to be neighborhood property if it is contiguous with exempt-purpose property or would be contiguous except for the interposition of a road, street, railroad, stream, or similar property. If the acquired property is not contiguous with the existing exempt-function property, it can still be considered neighborhood property if it is within one mile of the exempt-function property and the facts and circumstances of the particular situation make the acquisition of contiguous property unreasonable. Such facts and circumstances include the availability of land and the intended future use of the land.[155]

After the first five years of the ten-year period, an organization must establish to the satisfaction of the IRS that the acquired property will be used in furtherance of the organization's exempt purpose prior to the expiration of the ten-year period. This is done by showing a definite plan detailing a specific improvement and a completion date, and some affirmative action toward the accomplishment of the plan. The request for a ruling must be forwarded to the IRS at least ninety days before the end of the fifth year after acquisition of the land.[156]

The neighborhood land rule applies to any structure existing on the property when it is acquired by the exempt organization or to the land occupied by the structure only if the intended future use of the property in furtherance of the organization's exempt purpose requires that the structure be demolished or removed in order to use the property in that manner.[157]

If the neighborhood land rule does not apply because the acquired property is not in the neighborhood of the other land used for an organization's exempt purposes, or because the organization fails to establish after the first five years of the ten-year period that the property will be used for exempt purposes, but the property is eventually used by the organization for its exempt purposes within the ten-year period, the property will not be treated as debt-financed property for any period prior to the conversion.[158]

SPECIAL RULES—UNRELATED BUSINESS TAXABLE INCOME OF SOCIAL CLUBS AND EMPLOYEES' ASSOCIATIONS

Special rules apply in the calculation of unrelated business taxable income of social clubs, exempt from taxation pursuant to Section 501(c)(7); a voluntary employees' beneficiary association, exempt from taxation pursuant to Section 501(c)(9); and a supplemental unemployment benefit trust exempt from taxation pursuant to Section 501(c)(17). In general, unrelated business taxable income for such organizations is the gross income of such organization, excluding any exempt function income, less the allowable deductions which are directly connected with the production of such income.[159] This means that social clubs and employees' associations are not taxed on their exempt function income.

Exempt function includes two elements: gross income received from members and set-aside income.[160] Gross income received from members of a social club includes amounts derived from membership dues, fees, charges, or similar amounts paid by members to the organization as consideration to the organization for providing those members, their dependents, or guests with goods, facilities, or services in furtherance of the exempt purpose of the social club.[161] Gross income from an employees' association includes amounts paid by members as consideration for the association's payment of life, sick, accident, or other benefits to those members, their dependents, or designated beneficiaries.

Set-aside income is income set aside by a social club or by an employees' association for a religious, charitable, scientific, literary, or educational purpose, or for the prevention of cruelty to children or animals.[162] In the case of an employees' association, set-aside income also includes those amounts which are set aside by the association for the payment of life, sick, accident, or other benefits.[163] Amounts to cover reasonable administration costs directly connected with any set-aside income may also be set aside by either type of organization.[164] If any amount of set-aside income is used for a purpose other than those permitted, the amount used will be treated as unrelated business taxable income in the taxable year in which it is used.[165]

All, or a portion of, the gain on the sale of exempt property of a social club or employees' association may be rolled over if, within a period beginning one year before the date of the sale and ending three years after the date of the sale, the organization acquires new property which is to be used directly in the performance of its exempt function.[166] Gain from the sale is recognized only to the extent that the sale price of the old property exceeds the purchase price of the new property.[167] Reasonable allocations are made in situations when property which is only partially used for exempt purposes is sold, or when the property which is purchased is used only partially for exempt purposes.[168] The destruction, theft, seizure, requisition, or condemnation of property is treated as a sale of property, and the construction or reconstruction of property is treated as a purchase of property.[169]

NOTES

1. IRC Sec. 511(a)(2)(A).
2. IRC Sec. 511(a)(2)(B) and Reg. Sec. 1.511-2(a)(2).
3. Id.
4. Reg. Sec. 1.513-1(a).
5. Reg. Sec. 1.513-1(b).
6. Id.
7. Id. and IRC Sec. 162.
8. Reg. Sec. 1.513-1(b).
9. Id.
10. Id.
11. Id.
12. Reg. Sec. 1.513-1(c)(1).
13. Id.
14. Reg. Sec. 1.513-1(c)(2).
15. Id.
16. Id.
17. Id.
18. Reg. Sec. 1.513-1(c)(2)(i).
19. Reg. Sec. 1.513-1(c)(2)(ii).
20. Id.
21. Id.
22. Id.
23. Reg. Sec. 1.513-1(c)(2)(iii).
24. Id.
25. Reg. Sec. 1.513-1(d)(1).
26. Id.
27. Reg. Sec. 1.513-1(d)(2).

28. Id.
29. Reg. Sec. 1.513-1(d)(3).
30. Id.
31. Rev. Rul. 78-43, 1978-1 C.B. 164.
32. Rev. Rul. 69-269, 1969-1 C.B. 160.
33. Rev. Rul. 68-375, 1968-2 C.B. 245.
34. Hi-Plains Hospital v. U.S., 670 F.2d 528 (5th Cir. 1982).
35. Rev. Rul. 74-399, 1974-2 C.B. 172.
36. Rev. Rul. 73-104, 1973-1 C.B. 263. See also IRS Publication 598; Reg. Sec. 1.513-1(b).
37. See IRS Publication 598.
38. Rev. Rul. 81-61, 1981-1 C.B. 355.
39. Rev. Rul. 81-62, 1981-1 C.B. 355.
40. Reg. Sec. 1.513-1(d)(4)(i).
41. Id. ex. 1.
42. Id. ex. 3.
43. Reg. Sec. 1.513-1(d)(4)(ii).
44. Id.
45. Id.
46. Id.
47. Reg. Sec. 1.513-1(d)(4)(iii).
48. Id.
49. Id.
50. Reg. Sec. 1.513-1(d)(4)(iv).
51. Id. ex. 1.
52. Id. ex. 2.
53. Id. ex. 3.
54. Reg. Sec. 1.512(a)-1(f)(1).
55. Reg. Sec. 1.513-1(d)(4)(iv) ex. 4.
56. Reg. Sec. 1.512(a)-1(f)(2)(i).
57. Reg. Sec. 1.512(a)-1(f)(6)(ii).
58. Reg. Sec. 1.512(a)-1(f)(3)(ii).
59. Reg. Sec. 1.512(a)-1(f)(2)(ii).
60. Reg. Sec. 1.512(a)-1(f)(2)(ii)(a).
61. Reg. Sec. 1.512(a)-1(f)(2)(ii)(b).
62. Reg. Sec. 1.512(a)-1(f)(3)(i).
63. Reg. Sec. 1.512(a)-1(f)(6)(i).
64. Reg. Sec. 1.512(a)-1(f)(3)(iii).
65. Id.
66. Reg. Sec. 1.512(a)-1(f)(4).
67. Reg. Sec. 1.512(a)-1(f)(5).
68. Reg. Sec. 1.512(a)-1(f)(6)(iii).

69. Reg. Sec. 1.512(a)-1(f)(2)(iii).
70. Reg. Sec. 1.512(a)-1(f)(7)(i).
71. Reg. Sec. 1.512(a)-1(f)(7)(ii).
72. Id. ex. 5.
73. Reg. Sec. 1.513-1(e)(1).
74. Reg. Sec. 1.513-1(e).
75. Reg. Sec. 1.513-1(e)(2).
76. Reg. Sec. 1.513-1(e)(3).
77. Reg. Sec. 1.513-5.
78. Reg. Sec. 1.513-6; IRS Sec. 501(e)(1)(A).
79. Id.
80. Reg. Sec. 1.513-6(c).
81. IRC Sec. 513(d).
82. Reg. Sec. 1.513-3.
83. Reg. Sec. 513-3(d)(1).
84. IRC Sec. 513(h)(1)(B).
85. IRC Sec. 513(h)(1)(A).
86. Reg. Sec. 1.512(b)-1.
87. Reg. Sec. 1.512(b)-1(a) and (b).
88. Id. To be discussed later in this chapter.
89. IRC Sec. 512(b)(1).
90. IRC Sec. 512(a)(5).
91. Reg. Sec. 1.512(b)-1(d)(1).
92. Reg. Sec. 1.512(b)-1(d)(2).
93. Reg. Sec. 1.512(b)-1(f).
94. Reg. Sec. 1.512(b)-1(e).
95. IRS Publication 598.
96. Reg. Sec. 1.512(b)-1(e)(2).
97. Reg. Sec. 1.512(b)-1(e)(3).
98. Reg. Sec. 1.512(b)-1(e)(4).
99. IRC Sec. 512(b)(10).
100. IRC Sec. 512(b)(11).
101. IRC Sec. 512(b)(12).
102. Reg. Sec. 1.512(b)-1(h)(2).
103. Reg. Sec. 1.512(b)-1(j).
104. Reg. Sec. 1.512(b)-1(c)(2)(ii)(a).
105. Reg. Sec. 1.512(b)-1(c)(2)(ii)(b).
106. Id.
107. Id.
108. Reg. Sec. 1.512(b)-1(c)(3)(iv).
109. Reg. Sec. 1.512(b)-1(c)(2)(iii)(a).
110. Reg. Sec. 1.512(b)-1(c)(2)(iii)(b).

111. Reg. Sec. 1.512(b)-1(c)(3)(iii).
112. Reg. Sec. 1.512(b)-1(c)(2)(iv).
113. Reg. Sec. 1.512(b)-1(c)(3)(v).
114. Reg. Sec. 1.512(b)-1(c)(5).
115. Reg. Sec. 1.512(b)-1(l)(1).
116. Reg. Sec. 1.512(b)-1(l)(4)(i)(a).
117. Reg. Sec. 1.512(b)-1(l)(4)(i)(b).
118. Reg. Sec. 1.512(b)-1(l)(4)(ii).
119. Reg. Sec. 1.512(b)-1(l)(5)(i).
120. Reg. Sec. 1.512(b)-1(1)(5)(ii). Debt-financed property provisions will be discussed later in this chapter.
121. Reg. Sec. 1.512(b)-1(1)(2)(i)(b).
122. Reg. Sec. 1.512(b)-1(l)(2)(i)(a) and (b).
123. Reg. Sec. 1.512(b)-1(l)(3)(i)(a) and (b).
124. Reg. Sec. 1.512(b)-1(l)(3)(ii).
125. Reg. Sec. 1.512(b)-1(l)(3)(iii) ex. 1.
126. Reg. Sec. 1.512(b)-1(l)(3)(iii) ex. 2.
127. Reg. Sec. 1.514(a)-1(a)(1)(ii) and (iii).
128. Reg. Sec. 1.514(b)-1(a).
129. Id.
130. Reg. Sec. 1.514(a)-1(a)(1)(v).
131. Reg. Sec. 1.514(b)-1(b)(1)(i).
132. Reg. Sec. 1.514(b)-1(b)(1)(ii).
133. Reg. Sec. 1.514(b)-1(b)(1)(ii)(a), (b), and (c).
134. Reg. Sec. 1.514(c)-1(a)(1).
135. Reg. Sec. 1.514(a)-1(a)(3).
136. Reg. Sec. 1.514(a)-1(a)(3)(iii) ex. 1.
137. Reg. Sec. 1.514(a)-1(a)(4).
138. Reg. Sec. 1.514(c)-1(a)(3).
139. Reg. Sec. 1.514(c)-1(a)(4).
140. Reg. Sec. 1.514(c)-1(b)(1).
141. Reg. Sec. 1.514(c)-1(b)(2).
142. Reg. Sec. 1.514(c)-1(b)(3)(i).
143. Reg. Sec. 1.514(c)-1(b)(3)(ii).
144. Reg. Sec. 1.514(c)-1(b)(3)(iii).
145. Reg. Sec. 1.514(c)-1(c).
146. Reg. Sec. 1.514(a)-1(a)(2)(i).
147. Reg. Sec. 1.514(a)-1(a)(2)(ii).
148. Reg. Sec. 1.514(b)-1(b)(2)(i).
149. Reg. Sec. 1.514(b)-1(b)(2)(ii).
150. Reg. Sec. 1.514(b)-1(b)(3) ex. 3 (a) and (b).
151. Reg. Sec. 1.514(b)-1(b)(4).

152. Reg. Sec. 1.514(b)1(b)(5).
153. Reg. Sec. 1.514(d).
154. Reg. Sec. 1.514(b)-1(d)(1)(i).
155. Reg. Sec. 1.514(b)-1(d)(1)(ii).
156. Reg. Sec. 1.514(b)-1(d)(1)(iii).
157. Reg. Sec. 1.514(b)-1(d)(3).
158. Reg. Sec. 1.514(b)-1(d)(2).
159. IRC Sec. 512(a)(3)(A).
160. IRC Sec. 512(a)(3)(B).
161. Id.
162. Id.
163. Id.
164. Id.
165. Id.
166. IRC Sec. 512(a)(3)(D).
167. Id.
168. Id.
169. IRC Sec. 512(a)(3)(D).

5

Private Foundations

INTRODUCTION

As discussed in Chapter 2, the Section 501(c)(3) organization is the broadest type of tax-exempt organization. It is also the most desirable classification because the contributions it receives are tax deductible. In order to prevent 501(c)(3) organizations from using tax-deductible contributions to further the private interests of an organization's donors, founders, or managers, the Internal Revenue Code subdivides the 501(c)(3) classification into two broad categories, private foundations and organizations other than private foundations. Private foundations typically have a restricted base of support; consequently, they are prohibited from engaging in certain transactions that have the potential of benefiting closely related parties (such as substantial contributors) rather than the public at large. In addition, there are stricter limits related to the deductibility of contributions made to private foundations versus other 501(c)(3) organizations. As a general rule, contributions made to a private foundation are deductible only to the extent that they do not exceed 30 percent of adjusted gross income. The corresponding threshold for a 501(c)(3) organization which is not classified as a private foundation is 50 percent. Also, to ensure that foundations are responsive to the public interest, they are required to maintain a minimum level of charitable expenditures. If private foundations engage in prohibited transactions and/or if they fail to maintain specified levels of charitable expenditures, they are subject to a series of excise tax sanctions that can ultimtely result in termination of the foundation.

The purpose of this chapter is to discuss the definition of the term private foundations within the meaning of applicable code sections and to explore matters relating to permitted/prohibited activities and the excise taxes imposed thereon. This chapter will also address the voluntary processes by which a private foundation can terminate its status and resume operations without the restrictions imposed upon private foundations.

PRIVATE FOUNDATIONS DEFINED

Internal Revenue Code Section 509 defines the term private foundation. The manner in which private foundations are defined is pervasive; private foundations are defined by default. All 501(c)(3) organizations are presumed to be private foundations unless they fall into one of four categories. Internal Revenue Code Sections 509(a)(1) through 509(a)(4) describe the four exceptions. Nonprivate foundations are defined as:

- Charitable organizations described within IRS Code Section 170, Charitable Contributions and Gifts;
- Organizations supported by the general public through grants, gifts, contributions, and gross receipts from amounts realized in connection with the performance of activities consistent with the organization's exempt purpose;
- Organizations that are operated in connection with and/or are supervised or controlled by a charitable organization or a publicly supported organization; and
- Organizations which are operated exclusively for testing public safety.

Public Charities—Code Section 509(a)(1)

Public charities are defined in Internal Revenue Code Section 170 and are excluded from private foundation classification under IRS Code Section 509(a)(1). In general terms, this code section defines what contributions are deductible from gross income in terms of the attributes of the recipient organization. For purposes of determining whether or not an organization can be excluded from private foundation classification, the deductibility of the contributions it receives is the determining factor. Generally, if the contributions an organization receives are deductible from the gross income of the donor pursuant to Code Section 170, the organization is deemed to be a public charity, and is therefore excluded from private foundation classification under Code Section 509. Organizations described in Code Section 170 that are excepted from private foundation classification include:

- A church or a convention or association of churches;
- An educational organization which normally maintains a regular faculty and curriculum and normally has a regular enrolled body of pupils or students in attendance at a place where its educational activities are regularly carried on;
- An organization that normally receives a substantial amount of its support (exclusive of income received in connection with the performance of an organization's exempt activities) from the federal government, a state government, or from the general public; and
- A governmental unit.

Internal Revenue Code Section 170 describes two other types of organizations but these organizations are not excepted from private foundation classification under Code Section 509(a)(1). The reasons are rather obvious. Code Section 170(b)(vii) permits the deductibility (up to specified limits) of contributions to private foundations; by mere definition, private foundations cannot be excluded from private foundation classification. Similarly, Code Section 170(b)(vii) permits the deductibility of contributions to publicly supported organizations (Code Section 501(a)(2)) and supporting organizations (Code Section 509(a)(3)); exclusion from private foundation status under Code Section 509(a)(1) would be redundant.

The respective definitions of churches and educational institutions for purposes of both Code Sections 170 and 509 are rather straightforward. The definition of charitable organizations, that is, organizations that normally receive a substantial amount of their support from governmental agencies and the general public, requires an expanded discussion. There are specific tests that must be applied to determine if, in fact, a substantial level of external support is normally received by the organization. The regulations address the issue by specifying the term "substantial" to mean at least one-third. There are specific guidelines to follow when applying the one-third public support test. There are also limitations with respect to what can be considered public support with regard to funds received from governmental and private sources. The calculation in itself is simple. A fraction is created; the numerator of the fraction includes all sources of public support (subject to the limitations discussed below), and the denominator of the fraction includes all sources of support exclusive of income realized from the performance exempt activities unless the performance of the activities is coincidental with the receipt of certain grants.

The numerator of the fraction consists of government grants and public contributions and gifts. In order to ensure that the organization serves a public (versus a private) interest, there is a limitation with respect to the level of includable contributions from nongovernmental units. Generally, amounts received from private donors are includable only to the extent that they do not exceed 2 percent of the organization's total support base. Amounts in excess of the 2 percent ceiling are included within total support but excluded from public support when developing the fraction to test the relative level of public support.

When computing an organization's level of public support, extraordinary and/or unusual grants can sometimes be afforded special treatment so as to neutralize any distorting effect that they might have. Large, unusual, and/or unexpected amounts may be excluded from both public support and total support if they were received in connection with the organization's public purpose and if the large/unusual nature of the amount distorts the results of the underlying calculation. There are numerous other facts and circumstances that apply when considering the exclusion of large and unusual grants and contributions.

It should be noted that income realized from the performance of an organization's exempt activities (other than grants and contributions) is excluded from both the numerator and the denominator of the fraction. However, if such income is disproportionately high, the results of the calculation may be invalid with respect to qualifying for exclusion from private foundation classification under Code Section 509(a)(1). Organizations that rely heavily on income from the performance of exempt activities are generally subject to the public support tests associated with excepted organizations described in Code Section 509(a)(2).

The public support determination with respect to exclusion from private foundation classification pursuant to Code Section 509(a)(1) is based upon what is normally received. Regulation 1.170A-9(e)(4)(i) addresses this subject. The support determination is made on an aggregate basis over a four-year period—an organization is considered to have met the one-third public support threshold for the current tax year if, on an aggregate basis, public support exceeded the one-third threshold for the immediately preceding four tax years.

When computing the relative level of public support, investment income must be considered. Gross investment income that an organization realizes in the course of its business is included within total support but excluded from public support.

Regulation 1.170A-9(e)(3) provides a means by which an organization can forego compliance with the one-third requirement by meeting an alternate facts and circumstances test. In order for this test to be applicable, the organization must first be able to demonstrate that at least 10 percent of its support is derived from government funding and/or other public sources. The 10 percent floor is based upon "normal" receipts, that is, four tax years immediately preceding the current tax year on an aggregate basis. The organization must also be able to demonstrate that it has an ongoing program of fund solicitation and that its services and/or facilities are readily available to the general public. One other circumstance to be considered is the composition of the organization's governing body; a favorable determination is more likely if the governing body is composed of members representing a broad cross section of the community which the organization serves.

Publicly Supported Organizations—Code Section 509(a)(2)

Internal Revenue Code Section 509(a)(2) excepts from private foundation classification those organizations that have a broad public appeal but, by virtue of their income base, do not qualify for private foundation exclusion under the public support tests associated with 509(a)(1) Public Charities. The distinction between the two exclusions involves the treatment of income realized in connection with the performance of exempt functions. Organizations excepted from private foundation classification under Code Section 509(a)(1) rely heavily on government grants and contributions from the general public. Organizations that rely to a greater degree on income related to the performance of exempt functions and to a lesser degree on government grants and contributions are subject to a separate set of public support tests. These tests are described in Internal Revenue Code Section 509(a)(2). There are two support tests that must be applied.

The first test measures public support as a percentage of total support (similar to the 509(a)(1) Public Charity); however, the composition of the support components differs. Regardless of the composition of the components of support, organizations seeking exclusion from private foundation classification under Code Section 509(a)(2) must still demonstrate a public support factor of at least 33.3 percent.

When computing the level of public support, grants, gifts, and contributions are includable as public support and as total support. In addition, gross receipts from admissions, sales of merchandise, performance of services, or furnishing of facilities are also includable (subject to the limitations discussed below) if these receipts are derived from a trade or business related to the organization's exempt purpose.

The public support test for the 509(a)(2) exclusion is designed to ensure that the excepted organization serves a broad cross section of the community; there are certain restrictions with respect to the includability of certain components of public support. Amounts received from any one organization are includable in public support only to the extent that they do not exceed the greater of $5,000 or 1 percent of the organization's total support for the tax year. In addition, the amounts received must be from persons other than disqualified persons within the meaning of Code Section 4946 (see discussions on disqualified persons later in this chapter).

The second test that must be satisfied for the Section 509(a)(2) exclusion relates to the relative level of the organization's investment income and the amount of unrelated business taxable income that it receives. In applying this test, a floor is imposed limiting the combined amount of investment and unrelated business taxable income that an organization can have and still be excluded from private foundation classification. Generally, an organization can have no more than one-third of its support from these combined sources.

In order for an organization to qualify for exclusion from private foundation classification under Code Section 509(a)(2), both of the support tests discussed above must be satisfied. As was the case with the 509(a)(1) exclusion, support is measured by what is "normally" received. Organizations are deemed to have satisfied the support test for the current tax year if, on an aggregate basis, they meet the test for a four-year period preceding the current tax year.

Support Tests—Tax versus Accrual Accounting

The application of the support tests relating to both the 509(a)(1) and 509(a)(2) exclusions depart from generally accepted accounting principles. The tests are applied on the basis of amounts "normally" received. Income accruals (amounts earned but not received within an accounting period or tax year) are not includable in support determinations. This consideration may require an organization to implement additional bookkeeping procedures to monitor compliance. This is particularly true if the organization's public support base is near the minimum threshold.

Supporting Organizations—Code Section 509(a)(3)

Internal Revenue Code Section 509(a)(3) defines a third excludable category with respect to private foundation classification. Organizations described in this code section are not subject to the support tests associated with public charities or publicly supported organizations under the presumption that they are organized, operated, and controlled by either a public charity or publicly supported organization. The language of Section 509(a)(3) is quite clear with respect to describing the exclusion. An organization is considered a supporting organization if:

- It is organized and operated exclusively for the benefit of a public charity or a publicly supported organization;
- It is supervised and controlled by either a public charity or a publicly support organization; and
- It is not controlled by one or more disqualified persons (see discussions later in this chapter) other than a foundation manager and other than a public charity or publicly supported organization.

It should be noted that an organization can qualify as a supporting organization if it is organized/operated for and supervised by an exempt organization described in Sections 501(c)(4), (5), or (6) which would meet the support tests associated with public charities or publicly supported organizations.

In order to qualify as a supporting organization under Section 509(a)(3), an organization must meet certain organizational and operational tests in order to determine whether or not it is organized and operated for the benefit of a public charity or publicly supported organization. The regulations also address the meaning of operated, supervised, and controlled by.

Organizational Tests. The applicable organizational tests are described in Regulation 1.509(a)(4). The organizational considerations relate to the supporting organization's articles of organization. Generally, for the organizational tests to be met, the articles must:

- Limit the purpose of the organization to one or more of the purposes set forth in Section 509(a)(3), that is, the articles must limit the organization's activities with respect to ensuring that such activities benefit a public charity or publicly supported organization, or that the activities are performed for or carry out the purpose of one or more of these organizations;
- Not expressly empower the supporting organization to engage in activities which are inconsistent with its stated purpose;
- Identify the publicly supported organizations on whose behlaf the supporting organization will be operated; and
- Not expressly empower the supporting organization to operate, support, or benefit other than those organizations specified within the articles.

There is one point of clarification with respect to the organizational tests described above. Generally, the name of the supported organization must be specified within the articles. In some cases, however, the supported organization does not have to be expressly identified. If an organization supports several similar types of organizations, for instance all universities within a state, the name of each individual institution need not be specified. It is sufficient if the articles state that the organization is formed to support all of the universities within the geographic boundaries of the state. There are also other factors to consider when evaluating the need to specify the name of the supported organization. One of these factors relates to the historical relationship between the supported and supporting organization and the manner in which this relationship manifests itself publicly. The name of the supported organization does not need to be expressly identified if there has been a traditional relationship between the supported and the supporting organization and the common interests of the organizations are well established through their respective identities.

Operational Tests. The supporting organization must engage in activities that support or benefit the supported organization(s) specified within the supporting organization's articles. This does not necessarily mean that the supporting organization must limit its activities to making payments or providing facilities/services to the supported organization. The operational tests can still be met if payments are made or services are provided to an unrelated organization if the unrelated organization is in a class that is generally benefited by the supported organization. A supporting organization is not required to turn over its income to the supported organization to meet the operational test. A supporting organization may use its income to carry on independent activities as long as the activities benefit the supported organization(s).

Supporting organizations must be operated, supervised, or controlled by a public charity, a publicly supported organization, or an organization described within Code Sections 501(c)(4), (5), or (6) if the supported organization meets the tests associated with public charities or publicly supported organizations. The meaning of "operated, supervised, or controlled by" assumes that the supported organization has substantial control over the supporting organization's operations, policies, and procedures. Generally, control manifests itself when the officers and/or directors of the supporting organization are appointed by the supported organization and/or if they serve in a dual capacity in both organizations.

Organizations Organized and Operated Exclusively for Testing Public Safety—Code Section 509(a)(4)

The last type of organization that is excluded from private foundation status is an organization that is organized and operated exclusively for testing public safety. The three key terms are organized, operated, and exclusively. There is little authoritative literature available with respect to the meaning of these three terms. The absence of regulations and/or other guidelines addressing the 509(a)(4) exclusion suggests that a literal interpretation be applied to the language contained in the Internal

Revenue Code. In making a determination as to whether an organization qualifies for exclusion from private foundation classification under Section 509(a)(4), one may use the articles of organization as the primary point of reference.

Private Operating Foundation

Certain private foundations can qualify as private operating foundations. Private operating foundations differ from other foundations in that they do not routinely award grants to other 501(c)(3) organizations; private operating foundations utilize their respective resources to perform a specific exempt function and/or to offer specific services consistent with their exempt purposes. Because of the operational nature of a private operating foundation, it is not subject to excise taxes on failure to distribute income (see discussions on failure to distribute income later in this chapter). However, it is generally subject to all other restrictions and excise taxes associated with private foundations.

To qualify for private operating foundation status, an organization must meet the criteria specified in Code Section 4942. All private operating foundations must meet a standard income test. In addition, one of three other tests must be satisfied. These tests are the asset test, the endowment test, and the support test.

The Income Test. The income test requires that a private operating foundation make qualifying distributions, in connection with the performance of its exempt activities, equal to at least 85 percent of the lesser of its adjusted net income or its minimum investment return. Qualifying distributions are amounts paid to accomplish the exempt purpose of the organization or amounts paid to purchase assets used to perform the organization's exempt function. Payments to disqualified persons and/or to organizations controlled by the foundation are not considered qualifying distributions.

For purposes of the income test, the term adjusted net income is not synonymous with the accounting definition of net income. Adjusted net income is defined as gross income adjusted for certain modifications less total deductions adjusted for modifications. Modified gross income does not include gifts, grants, and/or contributions but does include income realized in connection with an unrelated business. Gross income also includes interest received on government obligations and short-term capital gains. Long-term capital gains are excluded from gross income. Gross income also includes any unused amounts that had been set aside for projects associated with qualifying distributions. Deductions generally consist of those normal business expenses recorded in the organization's accounting cycle; however, there are a few adjustments. Expenses associated with the acquisition of property that is used for nonexempt purposes are not allowed as deductions for purposes of the income test. Also, charitable contributions are not considered deductions.

Net investment income is defined as 5 percent of the excess of all assets' fair market value over the indebtedness incurred in connection with the purchase of the assets.

The Asset Test. In order to satisfy the asset test, 65 percent or more of an organization's assets must actively be used in the performance of the organization's exempt function, or 65 percent of the assets must consist of stock in a corporation that is controlled by the foundation. For purposes of satisfying the 65 percent threshold, any combination of these two requirements is acceptable.

The Endowment Test. In order to satisfy the endowment test, qualifying distributions must equal a minimum of two-thirds of an organization's minimum investment return.

The Support Test. Three criteria must be met for an organization to meet the support test. First, a minimum of 85 percent of an organization's support (exclusive of investment income) must be received from the general public; 5 percent of this amount must be received from unrelated exempt organizations. Second, no more than 25 percent of an organization's support can be received from any one exempt organization; and last, no more than 50 percent of an organization's support can be from investment income.

The Concept of Normally Received. The tests associated with private operating foundation classification are based upon what is "normally received." A four-year reference period is used to establish what is normally received. The income test and one of the three remaining tests must be satisfied for three years out of a four-year period. The four-year reference period includes the current tax year and the three tax years immediately preceding the current tax year. For newly created organizations, there is a modification of the three-out-of-four-year rule. A newly created organization will be treated as a private operating foundation if it meets the applicable test in the first year of its existence; thereafter, until a full four-year reference period is established, the tests must be satisfied in each subsequent year.

Exempt Operating Foundations. Under certain circumstances, private operating foundation can be classified as an exempt operating foundation. Exempt operating foundations are defined as private operating foundations which are exempt from taxes on net investment income (see discussions on tax on net investment income later in this chapter). To be considered an exempt operating foundation an organization must satisfy four criteria. First, it must be a private foundation. Second, it must be publicly supported. For purposes of determining whether or not an organization is publicly supported, the support tests associated with 509(a)(1) or 509(a)(2) apply. Generally, public support must be demonstrated for a minimum of ten years; an organization will be deemed as being publicly supported if it was a private operating foundation on 31 January 1983 or its last tax year prior to 1 January 1983. The third test involves the composition of the organization's governing body. The governing body (board of directors, and so on) must represent a broad cross section of the general public. Broad public representation is presumed to exist if at least 75 percent of the individuals making up the governing body are not disqualified persons (see disqualified person defined later in this chapter). The last test associated with exempt operating foundations relates to the organization's officers; exempt operating foundations may have no officers who are disqualified persons (other than a foundation manager).

DISQUALIFIED PERSON DEFINED

The term "disqualified person" has been used in conjunction with the several of the previously discussed tests applicable to private foundation classification. The term will also be used in the remaining discussions of this chapter. A disqualified person can be described, in general terms, as an individual or organization that is in a position to exercise substantial influence over the operations of a private foundation. Restrictions are imposed upon private foundations with respect to dealing with disqualified persons to prevent the disqualified person from using the organization for private benefit. Internal Revenue Code Section 4946, Definitions and Special Rules, defines disqualified persons as one of the following:

- A substantial contributor;
- A foundation manager;

- An owner of more than 20 percent of the total combined voting power of the corporation or the profits interest of a partnership that is a substantial contributor;
- A member of the family of a substantial contributor, a foundation manager, or a 20 percent owner of an organization that is a substantial contributor, a foundation manager, or other disqualified person; or
- A government official (only for purposes of self-dealing and the restrictions related thereto).

Substantial Contributors

Substantial contributors are deemed to be disqualified persons under the presumption that the amounts they contribute to the foundation permit them to exercise substantial influence over the operations of the foundation. A substantial contributor is defined as a person, corporation, trusts, or other organization that contributed or bequeathed more than $5,000 to the foundation, if the amount contributed, in any given tax year, exceeds 2 percent of the contributions or bequests received by the foundation. In most cases, once a person or organization becomes a substantial contributor, that person or organization will remain a substantial contributor regardless of future levels of support provided by that person or organization. There are, however, certain circumstances where a person or organization can escape substantial contributor status. A person or organization that was previously determined to be a substantial contributor will not be considered a substantial contributor for a given tax year if:

- That person or organization has not made any contributions for the past ten years, and
- That person or organization was not a foundation manager for the past ten years, and
- The IRS determines that prior contributions were insignificant with respect to the total contributions received by the foundation.

Section 501(c)(3) organizations that are excluded from private foundation classification under code sections 509(a)(1), Public Charities, 509(a)(2), Publicly Supported Organizations, and 509(a)(3), Supporting Organizations, are not considered to be substantial contributors even though they may have contributed amounts exceeding the specified levels.

Foundation Managers

For purposes of determining disqualified person status, a foundation manager is defined as:

- An officer, director, or trustee of a foundation, or
- An employee having substantial responsibility and authority with respect to committing the foundation to particular policies and/or commitments.

Family Members

Family members of disqualified persons are themselves considered disqualified persons. Family members include spouses, children, legally adopted children, grandchildren, great grandchildren, and spouses of children. Brothers and sisters are not considered family members with respect to disqualified person determinations.

Government Officials

Under certain circumstances government officials are considered disqualified persons. These circumstances relate exclusively to acts of self-dealing between private foundations and disqualified persons (see discussions later in this chapter). For self-dealing determinations, a government official is a disqualified person if:

- He holds an elected office in the executive or legislative branch of the United States government;
- He is a presidential appointee in the executive or judicial branch of the United States government;
- He holds a position in the federal government which is listed in Schedule C of Rule VI of the Civil Rights Rules, or the compensation received from the position held is equal to or exceeds the lowest rate prescribed for Federal job grade GS-16;
- He holds a position within the House of Representatives or the Senate and receives annual compensation in excess of $15,000;
- He holds an elective or appointed office in any state, possession of the United States, or the District of Columbia if the annual compensation received in connection with the office exceeds $20,000; or
- He holds a position as an executive assistant or secretary to any of the above.

The definition of government official described above appears to be rather all-inclusive. There is, however, a distinction between government official and public employee. The distinguishing factor involves an individual's ability to establish policy independently. Generally, the absence of the ability to establish and/or influence policy determinations substantially indicates that an individual is a public employee rather than a public official.

ACTS OF SELF-DEALING

Private foundations, regardless of whether they qualify as private operating foundations and/or exempt operating foundations, are prohibited from engaging in certain transactions with disqualified persons. Prohibited transactions, acts of self-dealing, are defined in Code Section 4941. In general terms, there are seven broad categories of self-dealing transactions:

- The sale or exchange of property between a private foundation and a disqualified person;
- The leasing of property between a private foundation and a disqualified person;
- Loan transactions executed between a private foundation and a disqualified person;
- The furnishing of goods, services, or facilities by a private foundation to a disqualified person or vice versa;
- The payment of compensation (including reimbursement of expenses) by a private foundation to a disqualified person;
- The use of a private foundation's income (either by direct transfer or use of assets) by a disqualified person; and
- Payments to a government official by a private foundation.

There are specific transactions that are excepted from the prohibitions against self-dealing. Under certain circumstances, a private foundation may provide goods, services, and/or facilities to a disqualified person. Similarly, private foundations may, in certain instances, make compensation payments to or reimburse the expenses of a disqualified person. Also, there are instances where amounts paid by a private foundation to a government official are not considered acts of self-dealing. Finally, certain lease transactions are excluded from the prohibitions against self-dealing.

A private foundation may provide goods, services, or facilities to a disqualified person if it does so on a nondiscriminatory basis with respect to similar transactions executed with the general public; the goods, services, or facilities provided to the disqualified person must be related to the private foundation's exempt purpose.

Compensation payments or expense reimbursements made by a private foundation to a disqualified person are not considered acts of self-dealing if they are made for personal services rendered to assist the foundation in carrying out its exempt purpose. In order to be excepted from self-dealing, the payments cannot be excessive.

There are several types of payments to government officials that are excepted from the definition of self-dealing. These payments include certain prizes and awards, scholarships, annuities paid pursuant to qualified plans, contributions or gifts under $25, and payments for attendance at a conference conducted to further the foundation's exempt purpose. Also, payments made to government officials under employment contracts are excepted from the definition of self-dealing if the agreement was executed within ninety days of termination of government service.

A disqualified person is permitted to lease property or facilities to a private foundation if there is no charge associated with the lease. Under such arrangements, charges for services incidental to the lease (e.g., maintenance or janitorial services) cannot be made directly or indirectly to the disqualified person.

Taxes on Self-Dealing

Section 4941 of the Internal Revenue Code imposes a series of excise tax sanctions on self-dealing transactions. There is an initial tax imposed, and if the acts of self-dealing are not corrected within a specified time period, additional taxes will be imposed. Excise taxes can be imposed on both the disqualified person and the foundation manager.

The initial tax imposed upon the disqualified person amounts to 5 percent of the amount involved for each taxable period. A companion tax of 2.5 percent is imposed upon the foundation manager who knowingly and willingly participates in the acts of self-dealing. For purposes of imposition of the excise tax, the taxable period is defined as the period beginning with the date of the self-dealing act and ending on the earlier of the date the notice of deficiency for the initial tax is mailed, the date the initial tax is assessed, or the date the correction of the act of self-dealing is completed.

If acts of self-dealing are not corrected within the taxable period (as defined in the preceding paragraph), an additional tax is imposed upon the disqualified person, and, under certain circumstances, upon the foundation manager. The additional tax imposed upon the disqualified person is 200 percent of the amount of self-dealing involved. This tax can be abated if the acts of self-dealing are corrected within the correction period. The correction period is defined as the period beginning on the day the act of self-dealing first occurred and ending ninety days after the date that a notice of deficiency for the additional tax is mailed. If the additional tax is imposed on the disqualified person, an additional tax of 50 percent of the amount involved can be imposed on a foundation manager(s), if the manager(s) refuses to correct the self-dealing act.

There is an upper limit to the excise tax that can be imposed upon the foundation manager; the maximum for the initial tax is $10,000 and the maximum for the additional tax is $10,000.

All acts of self-dealing must be corrected. Correction takes place by reversing the prohibited transactions to the extent necessary to restore the financial position of the foundation to the point at which it would have been had the transactions not taken place.

Repeated and flagrant violations with respect to acts of self-dealing can result in the foundation being involuntarily terminated by the IRS. Involuntary termination can result in a substantial termination tax in addition to the taxes previously discussed.

DISTRIBUTION OF INCOME

Internal Revenue Code Section 4942 imposes a tax on income that a private foundation fails to distribute within the current tax year or the year immediately succeeding the current tax year. The initial tax is 15 percent of the undistributed amount. The initial tax may be avoided if the foundation can demonstrate that its failure to distribute income was due to reasonable cause, and if it distributes the amount in question. There is an additional tax imposed, 100 percent of the undistributed amount, if the undistributed amount is not distributed by the end of the taxable period. The taxable period, as it relates to these requirements, begins on the first day of the tax year and ends on the date a notice of deficiency is mailed or the date the initial tax is assessed, whichever is earlier.

In order to comply with the income distribution requirements, a private foundation must make qualifying distributions for the period equal to or greater than their minimum investment return (defined earlier in this chapter). Qualifying distributions are amounts paid to accomplish the organization's exempt purpose or amounts used to purchase assets necessary to carry out the organization's exempt purpose. A foundation may, at its option, set aside certain amounts for future period distribution. These amounts are treated as qualifying distributions in the year they are set aside, not in the year they are spent. Funds may be set aside for a maximum of five years.

As discussed earlier in this chapter, private operating foundations are exempt from the taxes associated with the failure to distribute income. There are other exceptions to the requirements related to distribution of income. Certain long-term care facilities are not required to distribute income in accordance with Code Section 4942 if they have provided care continuously since 26 May 1979, and if they meet the endowment test associated with private operating foundations. Also, taxes will not be imposed if the failure to distribute income relates exclusively to the unintentional misvaluation of assets on the foundation's books.

TAXABLE EXPENDITURES

Internal Revenue Code Section 4945 imposes taxes on private foundations and on foundation managers if the foundation makes certain (taxable) expenditures. There are five categories of taxable expenditures:

- Amounts paid to carry on propaganda or to influence legislation;
- Amounts paid to influence the outcome of an election;
- Grants made to an individual for travel or study;
- Grants made to organizations other than organizations excepted from private foundation classification pursuant to Code Sections 509(a)(1), (2), or (3); and
- Amounts paid for activities other than those permitted in Code Section 501(c)(3) or to sponsor international amateur sports competition or to prevent cruelty to children or animals.

There are exceptions to these five categories of taxable expenditures. Generally, amounts spent in connection with lobbying activities are considered taxable expenditures; however, amounts spent for a nonpartisan analysis that is made available to the general public as well as to government bodies and/or officials are not considered lobbying expenditures. Similarly, a private foundation may participate in public discussions and/or discuss matters with public employees if the subject of participation or discussion does not relate to the benefits or lack thereof of a particular legislative proposal. Private foundations may engage in lobbying efforts if these efforts relate exclusively to the foundation's tax-exempt status and/or other matters relating to the foundation's existence.

Grants made to an individual for travel or study are generally considered taxable expenditures unless they are made on a nondiscriminatory basis in a manner approved by the IRS.

Under certain circumstances, grants made to individuals for travel and/or study are not considered to be taxable expenditures. First, the basis for awarding the grant must be nondiscriminatory and objective; the procedure under which the grant is awarded must be approved, in advance, by the IRS. Second, the grant must qualify either as a scholarship/fellowship for education at an institution which maintains a regular faculty, curriculum, and student body, or it must qualify as a prize or award to an individual recipient chosen from the general public. The second requirement will also be met if the purpose of the grant is to produce a specific report or to improve the literary, artistic, musical, scientific, or teaching skills of the recipient.

Taxes on Taxable Expenditures

If a private foundation makes a taxable expenditure, an initial tax of 10 percent of the amount spent is imposed upon the foundation. Foundation managers who knowingly participate in the transaction are subject to a 2.5 percent tax on the amount involved in the transaction. The tax imposed upon the foundation manager is subject to a ceiling of $5,000 per transaction. The initial tax can be avoided if the foundation can demonstrate that the expenditure was not made because of willful neglect and corrects the transaction no later than ninety days after a notice of deficiency for the additional tax (described below) is mailed.

An additional tax is imposed if the expenditure is not corrected by the earlier of the date the initial tax is assessed or the date the notice of deficiency for the initial tax is mailed. The additional tax imposed upon the foundation is 100 percent of the amount involved; the initial tax for the foundation manager is 50 percent of the amount involved subject to a $10,000 ceiling.

A taxable expenditure is considered to be corrected when all of the amounts that were expended are recovered or amounts are recovered to the fullest extent possible. When full recovery cannot be made, additional corrective actions will be dictated by the IRS. In this regard, the IRS may require the foundation to:

- Withhold any unpaid funds to a particular grantee;
- Cease making further grants to the payee;
- Improve controls with respect to expenditure responsibility procedures;
- Improve methods of selecting grantees; or
- Implement other actions as deemed appropriate under the circumstances.

JEOPARDIZING INVESTMENTS

Internal Revenue Code Section 4944 prohibits private foundations from making investments that can result in substantial financial losses which would prevent the foundations from carrying out their exempt purposes. There is no strict definition of the term "jeopardizing investment"; the term generally means highly speculative investments that can result in losses in excess of the original cost basis of the investment. Such investing activities include trading on margin, buying/selling commodity futures, buying "puts and calls," selling short, and buying warrants.

Taxes on Jeopardizing Investments

A private foundation is subject to an initial tax of 5 percent of the amount involved in purchasing jeopardizing investments. Foundation managers are also subject to a 5 percent tax if they knowingly and willfully participated in the transaction. The maximum initial tax for foundation managers is $5,000 per transaction. The initial tax is imposed on both the foundation and foundation manager for each tax year in the period beginning on the date the original investment was made and ending on the earlier of the date the funds are removed from jeopardy or the date the initial tax is assessed.

An additional tax is assessed (25% on the foundation and 5% on the foundation manager) if the funds are not removed from jeopardy on the earlier of the date the notice of deficiency for the initial tax is mailed or the date the initial tax is assessed. There is a ceiling on the additional tax that can be imposed upon foundation managers. The maximum additional tax is $10,000 for each jeopardizing investment.

EXCESS BUSINESS HOLDINGS

Internal Revenue Code Section 4943 prohibits private foundations and their related disqualified persons from holding more than 20 percent of the voting stock in an enterprise. The 20 percent limitation is based upon the combined holdings of the foundation and its disqualified persons. The 20 percent limitation also applies to holdings in unincorporated organizations such as partnerships or joint ventures. For unincorporated businesses, the 20 percent ownership is measured in terms of profit interest.

Taxes on Excess Business Holdings

An initial tax of 5 percent of the value of the excess holdings is imposed upon the foundation. The tax is imposed on the last day of each tax year the condition exists. When the condition involves two or more years, the final tax year is presumed to end on the date the notice of deficiency for the initial tax is mailed or the date the initial tax is assessed, whichever is earlier. For purposes of valuation, the tax is imposed on the largest amount of excess holdings during a given tax year.

There is an additional tax of 200 percent of the excess holdings amount if the condition is not corrected by the earlier of the date the initial tax is assessed or the date the notice of deficiency for the initial tax is mailed. The additional tax may be abated if the excess holding are disposed of no later than ninety days after the notice of deficiency for the additional tax is mailed.

INVESTMENT INCOME

Internal Revenue Code Section 4940 imposes an excise tax of 2 percent on a private foundation's net investment income. This tax applies to all private foundations except exempt operating foundations (discussed earlier in this chapter).

Net investment income is defined as gross income from interest dividends, capital gains (net of losses), rents, and royalties less any amounts paid in connection with earning and/or producing this income.

Under certain circumstances, a private foundation can qualify for a reduced tax rate of 1 percent. If the foundation was subject to excise taxes on self-dealing, failure to distribute income, excess business holdings, or jeopardizing investments at any time during the five tax years immediately preceding the current tax year, it cannot qualify for the reduced tax rate. If it is not subject to any of these taxes, it can qualify for the reduced rate if its qualifying distribution for the current tax year equals or exceeds an amount calculated applying the following formula:

> Assets × Average Five-Year Percentage Payout + 1% of Net Investment Income.

The average five-year percentage payout is calculated by dividing qualifying distribution for each of the five years by the foundation's assets. If the foundation qualified for the reduced tax in any year in the five-year base period, qualifying distributions in that year must be reduced by the amount of tax reduction when calculating the average percentage payout.

TERMINATION OF PRIVATE FOUNDATION STATUS

Once an organization is determined to be a private foundation, it remains a private foundation unless it is terminated in accordance with the provisions of Internal Revenue Code Section 507. Internal Revenue Code Section 507(a) addresses both voluntary and involuntary termination. Termination under the provisions of Section 507(a) subjects the terminating foundation to certain termination taxes which are addressed in Section 507(c). An organization wishing to avoid these taxes may wish to consider voluntary termination under Section 507(b)(1) or terminate under Section 507(b)(2), whereby it would be required to transfer its assets to another private foundation under an arrangement involving a liquidation, merger, or similar transaction.

An organization electing voluntary termination under Section 507(a)(1) must notify the appropriate IRS district director of its intent to do so. This statement must include a calculation of termination taxes due in accordance with the provisions of Section 507(c). If an abatement of these taxes is desired, the request must be included within the notification. If a partial abatement is requested, the amount of tax, net of the abatement requested, must be paid with the request to terminate. If the abatement is ultimately denied, the taxes must be paid immediately. If an organization wishes to continue to operate as an exempt entity after voluntary termination under Section 507(a)(1), it must reapply for tax-exempt recognition.

The IRS may, at its option, terminate a private foundation if the foundation willfully and flagrantly violates requirements involving self-dealing, distribution of income, taxable expenditure, jeopardizing investments, or excess business holdings. Such involuntary terminations can result in termination taxes under Section 501(c).

Voluntary termination of private foundation status under Section 501(b) is generally considered more desirable because the terminating foundation is not subjected to termination taxes. Code Section 507(b)(1) describes two methods of voluntary termination. Section 507(b)(2) describes a third option involving the transfer of assets to another private foundation.

Voluntary termination under Section 507(b)(1)(A) can be accomplished transferring a private foundation's assets to an organization described in Code Section 509(a)(1), that is, a public charity. The recipient organization must have been in existence, as a public charity, for a continuous period of at least five years. The terminating foundation is not required to notify the IRS of its intent to terminate if this method is chosen; however, if it wishes to continue in existence as a 501(c)(3) organization, it must reapply for tax-exempt recognition.

Voluntary termination under Section 507(b)(1)(B) requires the organization to demonstrate that it qualifies for exception from private foundation status, by meeting the requirements of organizations described in Sections 509(a)(1), (2), or (3) for sixty months. This determination can be made retrospectively or prospectively. Voluntary termination under Section 507(b)(1)(B) requires the organization to notify the IRS of its intent to terminate. An organization terminating private foundation status in this manner is not required to reapply for tax-exempt recognition. In cases of prospective determinations (advance rulings), failure to achieve the appropriate requirements of exception (over the sixty-month period) will result in the assessment of any and all applicable excise taxes for those years that the support thresholds and/or other requirements were not met. Organizations terminating private foundation status under Section 507(b)(1)(B) are not subject to the termination taxes described in Code Section 507(c).

Under Code Section 507(b)(2) an organization may terminate its private foundation status by transferring its assets to another private foundation in a liquidation, merger, recapitalization, or other similar transaction. In this type of termination, the transferring organization may be required to reapply for tax-exempt recognition if it wishes to continue its exemption under Section 501(c)(3).

Section 507(c)—Termination Taxes

Organizations whose private foundation status was involuntarily terminated by the IRS, and organizations requesting voluntary termination under Section 507(a), are subject to termination taxes. Under certain circumstances, these can be abated.

The termination tax is the lesser of the combined tax benefit associated with the 501(c)(3) organizational status or the value of the organization's net assets.

Generally, the combined tax benefit associated with an organization's 501(c)(3) status is the sum of the taxes that would have been imposed on substantial contributors had their contributions not been deductible and the taxes that would have been imposed on the foundation (since 1913) if the foundation had not been tax-exempt. One other item that impacts the combined tax benefit computation includes amounts received from other private foundations in the termination process. The value of the organization's net assets is the greater of the value of the net assets on the first day termination action was initiated or the value of the net assets on the day the termination was completed.

The IRS may abate the termination tax if one of two conditions is present. First, the termination tax may be abated if the foundation distributes all of its net assets to a public charity described in Section 509(a)(1), if the public charity has been in existence for at least five years. The tax may also be abated if the IRS is given adequate assurances that state proceedings will result in the charitable use of the organization's assets.

ORGANIZATIONAL CONSIDERATIONS—PRIVATE FOUNDATIONS

The governing instruments of a private foundation must contain all of the provisions required for 501(c)(3) organizations (see Chapter 2) and, in addition, they must contain special provisions addressing prohibitions on self-dealing, requirements to distribute income, restrictions on taxable expenditures, prohibitions against jeopardizing investments, and limitations with respect to excess business holdings.

If state law requires the foundation to operate in a manner consistent with the avoidance of the excise taxes imposed upon these transactions, these prohibitions and requirements do not have to be explicitly addressed within the governing instruments. However, to avoid potential questions and problems, the authors suggest that these considerations be addressed in the initial drafting of the organization's governing documents.

SUMMARY

All organizations recognized as being tax-exempt under Code Section 501(c)(3) are presumed to be private foundations unless they can demonstrate that they have broad public support and that they are responsive to the general public interest. Private foundations normally have a restrictive base of support; therefore, they are prohibited from engaging in certain transactions that may benefit substantial contributors and/or other parties. Private foundations are subject to restrictions involving transactions with substantial contributors, government officials, and foundation managers. Also, private foundations are required to maintain minimum levels of expenditures for charitable purposes. In addition, private foundations are subject to restrictions with respect to what type of expenditures and investments they can make; deviations from prescribed behavior in terms of the aforementioned restrictions can result in the imposition of a number of excise tax sanctions upon the foundation, foundation managers, and substantial contributors.

Once an organization establishes itself as a private foundation, it will continue to exist as a private foundation until it is terminated in accordance with the provisions of Internal Revenue Code Section 507. Under certain circumstances, private foundations are subject to substantial termination taxes. Avoidance of these taxes is possible if assurances can be given that the foundation's assets will continue to be used for charitable purposes.

6

Financial Considerations in Tax-Exempt and Other Nonprofit Organizations

INTRODUCTION

Tax-exempt and other nonprofit organizations are not unlike taxable, for-profit entities with regard to their respective needs for accurate, timely, and complete financial information. Decisions that are critical to an organization's continued existence are often dependent upon the integrity of the organization's financial data. Accordingly, due professional care must be taken in the design of an organization's accounting system as well as in the procedures employed for recording and summarizing financial transactions. All levels of management should possess a working knowledge of accepted techniques for recording financial transactions and be familiar with the concepts and objectives of financial accounting principles. The purpose of this chapter is to assist readers in designing a suitable accounting system and to provide guidance with respect to recording financial transactions. This chapter is also intended to provide a general overview of standard financial reporting formats.

The primary objective of accumulating, recording, and reporting financial information is to provide administrators, governmental agencies, and the general public with meaningful data concerning an exempt organization's operations and financial condition. The attainment of this objective is possible only when an organization adopts a systematic methodology with respect to its accounting system and then applies this methodology on a consistent basis.

THE DESIGN AND USE OF AN ACCOUNTING SYSTEM

Internal Controls

The first consideration in the design of an accounting system relates to internal controls. A poor system of internal controls and/or the absence of controls can result in erroneous and misleading financial information regardless of the accounting system's sophistication. Erroneous and misleading financial information more often than not leads to unsound fiscal decisions which can severely impede an organization's ability to accomplish its stated purpose. The discussions contained within this chapter are intended to give the reader a general overview of internal control systems and the importance of these systems with respect to the integrity of financial reports. Chapter 7 discusses the subject in depth and addresses specific implementation and evaluation techniques.

The term internal control is an all-encompassing term; it must be perceived in the broadest context. A good system of internal controls is based upon the general environment created by an organization's governing body. The control environment becomes the basis for the formation of specific control procedures and the acceptance of these procedures by the entire work force. The intentions of the governing body with respect to internal controls should be formally communicated to all organizational levels on a periodic basis. Methods of communication can vary. Any one and/or all of the following methods are recommended:

- A written policy statement asserting the organization's commitment with respect to establishing and maintaining a system of internal controls;
- A periodic reaffirmation of the policy statement published in employee publications;
- A formal procedures manual emphasizing control points within the workflow;
- Internal control workshops;

- A suggestion award program that includes awards for suggested control enhancements; and
- An independent statement in the organization's annual report attesting to the adequacy of internal controls.

The organization's commitment to establishing and maintaining a system of internal controls can also be communicated on an indirect basis. For instance, an organization's reporting structure can be designed in such a way as to provide for a continuous independent appraisal of the adequacy of controls. This can be accomplished by giving the internal audit executive direct reporting access to the organization's governing body.

There are two general types of controls in any system: accounting controls and administrative controls. Accounting controls are those designed to ensure that financial information is properly accumulated, recorded, and reported. Accounting controls govern direct information flows to the financial statements. A bank reconciliation is an example of an accounting control. Administrative controls are those which govern processes and procedures that indirectly impact the financial statements. A purchasing policy requiring supervisory approval for items costing over $100 is an example of an administrative control. The following example demonstrates the differences and similarities between accounting and administrative controls.

Example. A secretary wishes to purchase a calculator. She consults the organization's purchasing manual and determines that she is required to complete a requisition form and have the form signed by her superior (administrative control). She obtains the signature and forwards the requisition form to the purchasing department. The purchasing department is required to contact three vendors for price quotations (administrative control). The purchasing agent selects the lowest bidder and places a purchase order with the vendor. He mails a copy of the purchase order to the secretary and another copy to the accounting clerk. The accounting clerk records a payable on the books (accounting control). The calculator arrives and the secretary compares the make and model to the specifications on the purchase order (administrative control). She indicates that the calculator was received by signing the purchase order, then forwards the signed purchase order to the accounting clerk (administrative control). The accounting clerk places the signed purchase order in a hold file until the invoice arrives. Upon receipt of the invoice, the accounting clerk compares pricing information on the invoice with the corresponding information on the purchase order (accounting control). The accounting clerk requests his supervisor to approve payment (administrative control). A second accounting clerk prepares a payment check, has it signed by the treasurer (administrative control), and returns the signed check and invoice to the first accounting clerk. The first accounting clerk compares the amount on the check with the amount on the invoice (accounting control) and mails the check to the vendor. At the end of each month, the first accounting clerk compares the accounts payable balance on the trial balance to the total of open purchase orders in his possession; differences are investigated and resolved (accounting control).

As the preceding example illustrates, accounting and administrative controls generally work in conjunction with one another; they are not always mutually exclusive. There is, however, one common characteristic between accounting and administrative controls: their objective is either to *prevent* errors or irregularities or to *detect* errors or irregularities. For purposes of these discussions, the term "error" refers to an unintentional aberrant situation, while the term "irregularity" refers to an intentional aberrant situation. It is generally agreed that controls designed to prevent errors or irregularities are preferable to those that detect errors or irregularities after they have occurred.

The number and type of internal controls that an organization desires to include within the accounting system are purely subjective determinations. Too much emphasis on controls will slow processing times and place an unnecessary burden on administrative expenses. On the other hand, too little emphasis can lead to undetected errors and irregularities. The proper balance can only be determined on a case by case basis. Although there is no general consensus with respect to the number and types of controls an organization needs, it is generally agreed that a control should be installed only if the expected benefits exceed the cost. This concept, commonly called the concept of reasonable assurance, is accepted by most public accounting firms and internal auditors.

The Business Overview

The financial information needs of an organization depend upon a number of variables. These variables must be identified in order to determine the specific needs of an organization. Since no two organizations are alike, the variables impacting an organization's accounting needs will differ from organization to organization. In this regard, it is felt that the most expeditious way to identify an organization's unique attributes with respect to its accounting needs is to develop a comprehensive business overview. The following approach can be used for a newly created entity as well as an established entity wishing to reassess its financial informational needs.

The structure of a business overview should parallel traditional accounting classifications (revenue, expense, and so on). However, the environmental factors impacting the organization should be identified first. This is particularly true in a tax-exempt entity.

Environmental factors include, but are not limited to the following:

- The basis of the organization's exemption;
- Affiliations with other organizations;
- The relative size of the organization;
- Reporting requirements of regulating agencies;
- Reporting requirements of lenders; and
- Future business plans.

The basis of an organization's exemption should always be considered when assessing financial reporting needs. For instance, a teachers' retirement fund (exempt under Code Section 501(c)(11) will have needs substantially different from an organization whose sole purpose is to hold title to income-producing property and transfer its net earnings to another exempt organization (exempt under Code Section 501(c)(2)). Similarly, the needs of a private foundation differ significantly from a public charity even though both organizations are exempt under Code Section 501(c)(3). When analyzing the basis of an organization's exemption and the impact of the exemption on the accounting system, the financial executive should consult the applicable IRS regulations.

An exempt entity that is affiliated with another organization may wish to standardize accounting systems. In some instances this may be quite cumbersome, particularly when the operations of the two organizations are substantially different. If this is the case, a standardized accounting system may not be warranted and/or justified. If the two organizations have similar operations and/or one organization has the ability to control significantly the activities of the other, a standardized accounting system is probably warranted. In fact, a standardized system may be necessary to facilitate the preparation of consolidated financial statements.

The size of the organization will necessarily influence decisions relating to the accounting system. An important decision relates to whether or not an automated accounting system is needed. The authors believe that automated systems are warranted in all but the smallest exempt organizations. The major advantage of an automated accounting system is speed and accuracy. Although automated systems are preferable, there are additional control concerns that must be addressed if an automated system is chosen. These concerns involve input/output verification and data security. There must be controls to ensure that all information is input and accepted by the system. Although most software packages have controls built into them, manual input/output balancing routines and/or other verification controls should be designed to prevent undetected errors. Controls involving data security are critical; backup and recovery procedures must be established. In addition, controls to prevent unauthorized system access must be installed. These control concerns are the same regardless of whether a microcomputer or mainframe computer is used for processing.

Regulating agencies and lending institutions sometimes have reporting requirements that differ from tax reporting requirements and/or generally accepted accounting principles. There should be a mechanism to extract and/or accumulate data in various formats to accommodate the needs of agencies and lenders.

Future business plans should be identified prior to structuring a formal chart of accounts. Plans involving expansion, diversification, and/or specialization should be considered when designing and/or restructuring an organization's accounting system. In this regard, efforts should be made to ensure that the system is flexible enough to accommodate both expected and unanticipated operational and environmental changes.

The Chart of Accounts

A formal documented chart of accounts (reflecting the activities contained within an organization's overview) is the foundation of an organization's accounting system. A chart of accounts is nothing more than a codification of an organization's property, obligations, income sources, and costs. A chart of accounts enables an enterprise to record its daily activities on a consistent basis and to summarize the results of those activities in a manner that permits meaningful management review and analysis. In an exempt organization, the typical chart of accounts is divided into five broad categories: assets, liabilities, surplus, revenues, and expenses. Each of these categories is typically subdivided in a manner that combines similar elements within each classification. For example, assets (an organization's property) can consist of cash, short- and long-term investments, office furniture, electronic data processing equipment, accounts receivable, and other miscellaneous items of value. Similarly, an organization's liabilities (obligations) can include a variety of items such as trade accounts payable, short-term notes payable, long-term debt, and other miscellaneous commitments. An organization's surplus reflects the initial amount of its funding adjusted by operating results (excess of revenue over expense or vice versa). The revenue category includes all income sources such as government grants, private contributions and endowments, honoraria, membership fees, dues, member assessments, service fees, and other proceeds realized in connection with the performance of an organization's exempt function. The revenue category should also include unrelated business taxable income as well as income realized in connection with investment activities. The expense category is generally the broadest category within an organization's chart of accounts. The subdivisions of the expense category should be sufficiently detailed so as to identify the exact nature of the expense. For instance, salary costs should be classified in a separate account; professional fees paid to independent contractors (for example, attorneys, accountants) should be classified as professional service costs as opposed to salaries.

The relationships among the five chart-of-account classifications can be illustrated by the following equation:

$$\text{Assets} - \text{Liabilities} = \text{Surplus}$$

This equation (typically referred to as the accounting equation) depicts an organization's worth or its ability to perform its stated purpose on an ongoing basis. The excess of revenues over expense (profit) increases an organization's surplus and thereby enhances its ability to continue performing its exempt function; expenses in excess of revenues (loss) decrease surplus and impair an organization's ability to carry on its exempt purpose. Revenues increase an organization's assets (cash, accounts receivable) while expenses decrease assets (cash) or increase liabilities (accounts payable).

The codification process is a relatively simple task and is somewhat standardized within the accounting profession. Account classification can be identified with three-, four-, five-, or even six-digit identifiers known as account numbers. The number of digits used in the account number identification is a matter of individual preference; however, the degree of flexibility with respect to expanding a chart of accounts is directly proportionate to the number of digits used.

The first digit in an account number identifies the broadest classification, that is, asset, liability, surplus, revenue, or expense. It is suggested that the first digit of an account number be assigned in the following manner: the number one (1) should represent an asset account; liabilities should be identified with the prefix of two (2); surplus (the excess of assets over liabilities) should be identified with the prefix of three (3); and the first prefix digits used for revenues and expenses should be four (4) and five (5) respectively. There are variations to the preceding prefix assignments; however, for purposes of uniformity these assignments will be used throughout this text.

As previously stated, account numbers can vary in length. However, in order to simplify this specific model, a four-digit account will be used. The first two digits of the account number will be referred to as the prefix and the last two digits will be referred to as the suffix.

The second digit of an account number usually represents a broad subdivision within the basic account classification (asset, liability, etc.). For example, the prefix 10 may be used for cash assets, 11 for investments, 20 for accounts payable liabilities, and 21 for short-term debt obligations. The order of assignment for assets and liabilities typically reflects a systematic relationship between the various classifications. Assets are generally listed in order of liquidity. Liabilities are listed in the general order in which they mut be satisfied, that is, short-term (one year or less) versus long-term (greater than one year). Revenues and expenses are listed in order of their relative significance in terms of dollar volume. Surplus accounts are usually segregated in pools based upon anticipated or designated projects or use.

The suffix portion of the account number is the most specific indicator of the classification. For example, cash accounts may be designated in the following manner:

Petty Cash	1010
Cash—ABC Bank	1020
Cash—XYZ Bank	1021

Similarly, accounts payable can be designated as follows:

Trade Accounts Payable	2010
Intercompany Accounts Payable	2020

It is important to note that the preceding examples provide a degree of flexibility in terms of expanding an existing chart of accounts. For example, the codification of cash accounts can be expanded to accommodate twenty separate petty cash funds (account number 1010 through account number 1019) and eighty separate bank accounts (account number 1020 through account number 1099). The flexibility can easily be enhanced by expanding the number of digits used in the initial construction of the chart of accounts.

Exhibit 6-1 illustrates a chart of accounts that a typical exempt organization might use.

An exempt organization's chart of accounts can be more (or less) sophisticated than the chart in Exhibit 6-1; the degree of sophistication is dependent on the size and complexity of the organization.

Recording Transactions

An exempt organization's accounting system should provide a formal, consistent manner in which to record its financial transactions within the framework provided by the chart of accounts. Although financial transactions are expressed in monetary terms they do not necessarily involve the transfer of cash. The method of accounting prescribed by generally accepted accounting principles, the accrual method, requires that revenues be realized and recorded when earned and that expenses be recognized and recorded when incurred. Accordingly, the method chosen for recording transactions should accommodate compliance with this principle.

The recording of transactions requires the elementary application of standardized bookkeeping techniques and an understanding of how these techniques impact accounting reports.

Exhibit 6-1
Skyview Research Institute Chart of Accounts

Assets

1001	Petty Cash
1021	Cash - Skyview Bank
1022	Cash - Skyview Savings & Loan
1023	Cash - Pennybank
1101	Short-Term Investments
1110	Long-Term Investments
1201	Accounts Receivable - Grants
1211	Accounts Receivable - Contributions
1221	Accounts Receivable - Exempt Services
1231	Accounts Receivable - Other
1301	Accrued Interest Receivable - Short-Term
1310	Accrued Interest Receivable - Long-Term
1401	Prepaid Rent
1402	Prepaid Insurance
1501	Fixed Assets - Furniture & Fixtures
1502	Accumulated Depreciation - Furniture & Fixtures
1503	Fixed Assets - Equipment
1504	Accumulated Depreciation - Equipment

Liabilities

2001	Accounts Payable - Trade Creditors
2021	Accounts Payable - Federal Income Tax Withholdings
2022	Accounts Payable - FICA Withholdings
2023	Accounts Payable - State Income Tax Withholdings
2024	Accounts Payable - Local Tax Withholdings
2101	Accrued Payroll Tax Expense - FICA
2102	Accrued Payroll Tax Expense - Other
2103	Accrued Salaries
2201	Revenue for Future Periods

Surplus

3001	Unrestricted Surplus
3010	Restricted Surplus
3020	Designated Surplus

Revenues

4201	Revenues - Grants
4211	Revenues - Contributions
4221	Revenues - Exempt Services
4231	Revenues - Other
4999	Income Summary

Expenses

5001	Salaries, Wages, Overtime
5010	Employee Benefits
5020	Rent
5030	Repair & Maintenance
5040	Supplies & Printing
5050	Insurance
5060	Depreciation
5070	Postage
5080	Telephone
5090	Other Expense
5999	Expense Summary

Transactions should be recorded using the "double-entry" method of bookkeeping; each transaction is recorded in terms of a debit *and* a credit. Debits and credits can best be defined in terms of their impact on various account classifications. Debits increase asset and expense accounts while credits increase liability and revenue accounts. The converse of the preceding statement is also true. Inasmuch as credits increase revenues and debits increase expenses, their respective impact on surplus accounts (excess of revenues over expenses) is the same, that is, credits increase an organization's surplus while debits decrease surplus. The record of each transaction has at least four elements: a debit, a credit, an account number, and an amount. The following example illustrates both the accrual method of accounting and the double-entry method of bookkeeping.

Example. On 31 January 19xx, the Venus Research Foundation completed a thirty-day research project for the state of North Dakota. Under the terms of its agreement with the state, payment of $10,000 is to be made thirty days after submission of the final report. The appropriate entry for recording this transaction is as follows:

January 19xx

Debit Account 1221—Accounts Receivable Exempt Services	$10,000
Credit Account 4221—Revenues—Exempt Services	$10,000

In the above example, the entry recognizing revenue is recorded in January 19xx because that is the month in which the revenue was earned. The revenue is recorded on a current basis regardless of when cash is received. Recording revenue in this manner permits a meaningful comparison with respect to the corresponding expenses incurred in connection with earning this revenue (assuming expenses are recorded on a consistent basis) and provides management with meaningful data to measure performance.

Expenses, like revenues, should be recorded on a current basis (when incurred rather than when paid) in order to provide a meaningful comparison with the revenues.

Example. In January 19xx, WBST Communications Incorporated, a not-for-profit television station, rented certain facilities from a local department store for filming a documentary on adolescent shoplifting in the community. The documentary was funded by a $10,000 federal grant which will not be received until February 19xx. All production work, including filming, was completed in January 19xx. On 31 January 19xx, the department store submitted an invoice for $2,000. WBST Communications plans to pay this invoice in February 19xx. In this example, the following entries are appropriate:

January 19xx

To record award of federal grants:

Debit Account 1201—Accounts Receivable—Grants	$10,000

Credit Account 4201—Revenues—Grants	$10,000
To record the rental expense of temporary production facilities:	
Debit Account 5020—Rent	$ 2,000
Credit Account 2001—Accounts Payable Trade Creditors	$ 2,000
February 19xx	
To record receipt of federal grants:	
Debit Account 1021—Cash—Skyview Bank	$10,000
Credit Account 1201—Accounts Receivable—Grants	$10,000
To record payment of rent invoices:	
Debit Account 2001—Accounts Payable—Trade Creditors	$ 2,000
Credit Account 1201—Cash—Skyview Bank	$ 2,000

Journals. Entries such as those illustrated in the previous two examples should be recorded for each transaction in a formal record. This record is commonly called a journal. Each individual entry within a journal is called a journal entry. The most common type of journal is a summary journal. Summary journals are normally established for all cash transactions. For instance, a cash receipts journal is a multi-columm record which lists, in chronological sequence, all cash received during an accounting period (debits to cash). It contains information identifying the date of receipt, the party remitting the cash, and the account(s) (credits) to which the receipt applies. A cash disbursement journal contains similar information, that is, the date of disbursement, the amount (credit to cash), the payee, the check number, and the appropriate account distribution (miscellaneous debits). A payroll journal is similar to a cash disbursements journal except that the account headings for the distribution of amounts paid are unique to payroll transactions (salary expense, withholdings, advances, etc.). Summary journals can be prepared manually, or they can be maintained within an automated environment (microcomputer or mainframe). The use of summary journals facilitates the subsequent processing of raw financial data; only the totals need to be used in subsequent records. For example, the totals from the columns of a cash disbursement journal can be summarized in one entry as follows:

Credit Cash

Debit Accounts Payable—Trade Creditors

Debit Fixed Assets—Furniture & Fixtures

Debit Prepaid Rent

Debit Miscellaneous Expense.

It is important to note that each column of a summary journal should correspond to only one account.

Exempt organizations cannot rely exclusively on summary journals for recording individual transactions. The nature of the exempt organization as well as compliance with the accrual method of accounting prevent the exclusive use of summary journals. There are numerous transactions that occur both prior and subsequent to the exchange of cash. These transactions must be recorded in order to reflect properly an organization's financial performance and condition. The objective of these types of entries is to ensure the proper matching of revenues and expenses. Although it is impossible to identify all transaction types requiring individual (special) journal treatment, it is possible to describe briefly several common transactions and to suggest methods to record their impact on performance and financial position. Typical transactions requiring special journals involve recognition of revenues, acquisition of certain assets, and recognition of incurred expenses.

Recording Revenue. Organizations that rely heavily on government funding for specific projects, for example, research grants, should record revenue in a manner which reflects progress in completing the funded project. The easiest way to accomplish this is to provide for a series of entries involving cash movements and a separate series of entries involving (or reflecting) expended effort. The objective of the initial accounting entry is twofold:

1. To establish a receivable on the organization's books in order to permit the organization to control subsequent cash receipts; and
2. To recognize and reflect the organization's commitment to perform the tasks associated with the award.

As these objectives imply, the organization has acquired an asset (grant receivable) in exchange for a commitment to perform. In substance, the organization has a liability or an obligation to perform the tasks associated with the funded project. The entry to reflect this relationship is:

Debit Accounts (Grants) Receivable

Credit Unearned Income.

It should be noted that "unearned income" is a liability account because it reflects an obligation to expend funds (by performing the specified tasks) at a future date.

After this entry is recorded, the organization can record cash receipts using a summary journal to credit (reduce) the receivable. The liability associated with the obligation to perform should be reduced in a systematic manner that reflects actual progress in completing the project (not necessarily cash receipts). One such method is to measure progress in terms of task completion. For example, if during the first month one of five tasks is completed, 20 percent of the unearned income becomes earned; therefore, an entry can be reduced reducing the liability by 20 percent and recognizing the associated revenue:

Debit Unearned Income

Credit Revenue—Government Grants.

In most instances, however, recognizing revenues in terms of a percentage of project completion is not accurate. This is particularly true if some tasks require more intense manpower commitments (thus more expense) than other tasks. Revenue recognition should always be based upon a systematic method of measuring earnings in terms of resource use. Many exempt organizations routinely require their employees to record their individual time reports, by project, in order to make these determinations.

Occasionally, a parent of an exempt organization will contribute a relatively large sum to an exempt subsidiary for purposes of subsidizing the subsidiary's administrative expense burden. Transactions of this nature are common in the early years of an exempt organization's existence. Since these funds are not directly associated with a particular project and/or service (they are unrestricted), a rationale or policy must be established with respect to recognizing revenue associated with these funds. Since the funds are, in fact, unrestricted, an argument can be made for recognizing the entire amount of the contribution as revenue upon receipt. However, organizations that have adopted this practice have been subject to both internal and external criticism because of the distorting effect on interim financial reports. One method to avoid this criticism is to record the cash receipt as an unearned income liability and periodically to reduce this liability by recognizing revenue on the basis of time (e.g., straight-line over twelve months).

The revenue base of several exempt organizations consists of pledges from the general public. Currently, there is no hard and fast rule for establishing a receivable or recognizing revenue associated with pledges; the method of revenue recognition is dependent upon a number of variables such as:

- The nature and type of the pledge;
- The legal enforceability of the pledge;
- Standard industry practice; and
- The likelihood of the pledge materializing.

As a general rule, the receivable associated with pledges and the corresponding revenue should be recognized at the time the pledge commitment is made. There should, however, be a mechanism to "temper" the amount for realistic estimates of pledges that will not be received. This can be accomplished by establishing an account to offset the receivable; such an account is commonly referred to as a contra account. The mechanics of the necessary entries are as follows:

1. Debit the appropriate receivable and credit revenue in the aggregate amount of the pledge(s).
2. Credit a contra account (e.g., allowance for doubtful pledges) to reflect an estimate of pledges that will not materialize and reduce (debit) revenues accordingly.

The preceding practice will necessitate a certain amount of monitoring of subsequent cash receipts to ascertain the reasonableness of the estimate. If it is found that more pledges materialize than anticipated, additional revenue should be recognized by reducing (debiting) the contra account. The converse of the statement is also true.

Occasionally, pledges will be made for a time period exceeding the normal accounting cycle of one year. If this situation occurs, a determination should be made with respect to accounting for that portion of revenue attributable to future periods. As a general rule, the aggregate amount of the receivable can be recorded in the period the pledge is made; however, only the current portion of revenue should be recognized. The revenue associated with the remaining amount of the pledge should be deferred. This can be accomplished by crediting a deferred revenue account (a liability). This account can then be reduced by recognizing (crediting) revenue in the appropriate accounting period. Situations of this nature should be rare; they should arise only when donors specify an extended period with respect to amounts pledged.

Small, community-based exempt organizations may feel that it is unnecessary to record revenues in the manner suggested above. Typically, these organizations are geared toward specific public service and feel that they have little, if any, need to measure performance in terms of financial statistics. For example, a volunteer fire department may wish to record a receivable for the entire amount pledged in a community fund-raising drive. On the surface, this practice may appear acceptable but it can have undesirable consequences and potentially could jeopardize the financial stability of the organization. Decisions to make major capital asset acquisitions that are based upon unrealistically high pledge receivable balances may lead to a temporary cash crunch or even to insolvency.

Recording Fixed Assets and Depreciation. The majority of exempt organizations need certain fixed assets such as buildings, office equipment, and vehicles to perform their established exempt function. When acquisitions of this nature are expected to be used over several accounting periods, the expense associated with their acquisition should be recorded over the periods the assets benefit, that is, over the useful life of the assets. The basic entry is straightforward:

Debit Fixed Assets
Credit Cash.

The entry above can easily be recorded in a summary journal. Since the asset will be used in the operations of the exempt organization for earning revenue, and since use of the asset theoretically reduces its value over time, periodic expense entries should be recorded reflecting the reduction in value caused by the assets' use in the revenue earning process. This expense is referred to as depreciation. The entry to record depreciation expense is:

Debit Depreciation Expense
Credit Accumulated Depreciation.

The accumulated depreciation account should be included in the asset section of the chart of accounts; it is a contra account (an offset) to the fixed asset account.

There are several methods available to compute depreciation expense. In an exempt organization, the method used should be based solely upon management's assessment of the useful life of the asset and the manner in which the asset declines in value over time. By contrast, depreciation determinations in taxable organizations are often made based upon accelerated methods that are permitted by taxing authorities solely as a means of encouraging investment. The latter type of depreciation calculations generally do not reflect an asset's useful life or its realistic loss in value over time.

The simplest, most common, and probably the best way for an exempt organization to compute depreciation expense is to utilize the straight-line method. The straight-line method of depreciation assumes that an asset's decline in value occurs on a consistent basis over its useful life. For example, the expense associated with a personal computer configuration costing $5,000 may be recognized in five years by recording $1,000 per year in depreciation expense. At the conclusion of year five, the net book value of the personal computer would theoretically be zero; however, if the computer is still used, the original purchase price should remain on the books (in the fixed asset account). The true balance of the asset is zero because the expenses have been accumulated in the contra account which offsets fixed assets. Only when an asset is sold or scrapped should it be written off the books entirely.

For purposes of computing depreciation expense, the length of an asset's useful life is a variable that is assigned by management. Although some diligence should be exercised in assigning a useful life span to each asset, it is recommended that assets be grouped into useful life categories for purposes of consistency. For example, all motor vehicles can be treated as having a useful life of three years while office furniture can be assigned a five-year useful life.

In some instances, it is clearly obvious that an asset will be used or will be more productive in the first few years of its useful life and less useful or productive in the latter years. In these cases, management may wish to reflect the decline in value on an accelerated basis, that is, recognize greater amounts of depreciation in the earlier years of an asset's existence and lesser amounts in the remaining years. There are several methods available to reflect these types of situations. Two of the most common methods are the sum-of-the-years digits method and the declining-balance method. Both methods are recognized as acceptable within the accounting profession.

To calculate depreciation expense under the sum-of-the-years digits method, a fraction is developed for each year of an asset's useful life and is applied to the cost basis of the asset each year. The denominator of the fraction is the sum of the number of years of the asset's useful life. For example, the denominator for an asset having a useful life of five years is 15 (calculated by adding 1 plus 2 plus 3 plus 4 plus 5). The numerator varies; the numerator for the first year is the useful life, in this case five years. The numerator is reduced by one for each subsequent year. Hence, for a five-year asset costing $5,000, yearly depreciation expense is calculated in the following manner:

Year	Fraction	Historical Cost	Depreciation Expense
1	5/15	$5,000	$1,665
2	4/15	5,000	1,333
3	3/15	5,000	1,000
4	2/15	5,000	667
5	1/15	5,000	335
15			$5,000 Total Depreciation

As illustrated by the preceding example, depreciation expense is greater in the earlier years of an asset's life under the presumption of accelerated value loss caused by expected productive use, market factors, or a combination of both.

Another accepted method of calculating accelerated depreciation is the declining-balance method. This method is similar to the sum-of-the-years digits method in that it results in greater depreciation expense in the earlier years of an asset's useful life and less expense in the latter years. It is dissimilar to the sum-of-the-years digit method in that the rate of depreciation remains constant; the asset base to which the rate is applied is systematically reduced by the amount of prior years' depreciation throughout the calculation period. Assume that management feels that a five-year, $5,000 asset loses value at a greater rate than the straight-line method (20% per year) and even at a greater rate than the sum-of-the-years digits method. A depreciation model can be developed using the declining balance method to compute depreciation expenses in a manner consistent with management's expectations. The rate used must be greater than the straight-line rate; it is common practice to double the straight-line rate in using this method. Thus, the yearly depreciation expense for a five-year asset would be calculated by multiplying the adjusted value of the asset (cost less prior depreciation amounts) by 40 percent. The following table illustrates this concept for an asset costing $5,000 and having a useful life of five years.

Year	Depreciation Rate	Net Book Value	Depreciation Amount
1	40%	$5,000	$2,000
2	40%	3,000	1,200
3	40%	1,800	720
4	40%	432	173
5	40%	259	104
			$4,197

As illustrated by the above table, the asset still has "book value" ($803) at the conclusion of its useful life. The mechanics of this calculation will never permit the net book value to reach zero. If this method of depreciation is chosen, management may wish to continue with the calculation (in subsequent years) until the net book value is so small that recognizing the additional depreciation to depreciate the asset totally will not have a material effect, or to recognize the difference (in this case $803) as additional depreciation in the first few years of an asset's life. The authors recommend the latter alternative. The following continuation of the above example illustrates this recommendation.

Year	Declining Balance Depreciation	Additional Depreciation	Total Depreciation
1	$2,000	$ 268	$2,268
2	1,200	268	1,468
3	720	267	987
4	173	-	173
5	104	-	104
	$4,197	$ 803	$5,000

The methods of computing depreciation discussed in the preceding paragraphs assume that assets have no ''scrap'' value at the conclusion of their useful life. This assumption is followed by most practitioners and is recommended by the authors.

The accounting methodologies for asset acquisitions described in the preceding paragraphs relate exclusively to tangible property. Exempt organizations occasionally acquire intangible assets. Given the assumption that intangible assets benefit several accounting periods, it is necessary to record special journal entries after recording the initial cash outlay (as an asset) in a summary journal. Two common types of intangible asset acquisitions involve computer software and organizational costs. The expense associated with the use of intangible assets is called amortization. Intangible assets are amortized over the time period that they are expected to benefit. Most exempt organizations amortize intangible assets using the straight-line method. This practice is based on the assumption that the asset benefits all accounting periods equally. This appears to be a valid assumption given the absence of variables to the contrary. The journal entry for recognizing amortization expense varies slightly from the entry used to record depreciation. Amortization is not accumulated in a contra account; the expense (debit) is recognized by directly reducing (crediting) the appropriate asset.

Recording Expense. Due professional care should be exercised when recording expenses to ensure that they are recorded in the accounting period in which the expenses were incurred (rather than paid). Failure to record expenses in the proper accounting period will result in distorted financial results and could lead to erroneous conclusions with respect to evaluating specific projects and/or overall organizational performance. Although the administrative burden of accomplishing the preceding objective can be minimized through the proper use and maintenance of a cash disbursements journal and a payroll summary journal, special journals must necessarily be prepared for certain expenditures.

The columns of an organization's cash disbursement or payroll summary journal should accommodate as many accounts as possible without placing undue time and productivity constraints on the bookkeeping process. In order to avoid an otherwise large, cumbersome journal it is recommended that a miscellaneous account column, subdivided to show both account number and amount, be used for infrequently occurring expenditures. As cash disbursements are made, they should be charged or credited to the appropriate expense, asset, or liability account.

Payments made for current operating expenses such as utilities, supplies, maintenance, and so on, can be charged (debited) directly to the appropriate expense account in the cash disbursements journal. No further bookkeeping is required for these payments. At the conclusion of each interim and final (yearly) accounting period, a special journal should be prepared to recognize expenses associated with unpaid invoices by debiting the appropriate expense and crediting accounts payable. This entry should be reversed in the subsequent period. Payments for these invoices can then be charged (debited) directly to expense; the net impact to subsequent period expenses will be zero. This practice (reversing the accounts payable entry in the subsequent period) is recommended as a means of simplifying the bookkeeping process; the employee responsible for assigning account distributions to invoices will not have to make determinations with respect to whether or not an invoice was included in the accounts payable balance.

Payments are sometimes made for items that benefit future periods. Prepaids are considered assets because they represent rights to future products or services. Examples include rent and insurance. The initial expenditure should be recorded in the cash disbursements journal as a debit to the appropriate asset account, that is, prepaid rent, prepaid insurance. Special journals should then be prepared to reduce (credit) the asset and recognize (debit) the expense in the proper period. To facilitate this process, it is recommended that separate registers be maintained that contain details supporting the prospective distribution of the expenditure.

Payroll expenses can easily be recorded in a summary journal. Individual payroll checks are entered in the following manner: gross earnings are posted under the salary expense column (debit), withholdings are posted to the columns designated for the appropriate liability account (credits), and net pay is entered as a credit to cash. Subsequent payments made to satisfy withholding liabilities are then recorded in the cash disbursements journal as credits to cash and debits to the various withholding liability accounts.

There are several situations where expenses should be recorded even though there is no explicit demand for payment (such as an invoice). These situations generally involve payroll and payroll tax/fringe benefit transactions. Inasmuch as personnel costs generally comprise a significant portion of an exempt organization's expenses, a liability should be etablished reflecting incurred, unpaid expenses.

Unpaid salary expenses arise when the last payday in an accounting period occurs prior to the close of the accounting period. In effect, the organization has an obligation to pay the unearned salaries on the next payday. This liability is referred to as accrued salary expense. An estimate of this liability should be established and salary expense reflecting this liability should be recorded in the following manner:

Debit Salary Expense

Credit Accrued Salaries.

Since some employer-paid payroll taxes are based upon the level of salaries (employer's portion of social security and federal and state unemployment taxes), a liability should be established that corresponds to the unpaid salary accrual. This is simply a matter of applying the statutory percentage to the amount of the unpaid salary accrual (adjusted for established ceilings). Once the amount is determined, an entry recognizing payroll tax expense can be made by charging (debiting) the expense and crediting the accrued tax liability account. Inasmuch as it is a relative certainty that the unpaid salaries will be paid and expensed in the subsequent account period, the estimated salary accrual should then be reversed. The payroll tax expense accrual for unpaid salaries should also be reversed in the subsequent period.

Payroll taxes are not paid at the time that salaries and/or wages are paid; however, the paying organization incurs a liability when payroll checks are made available to employees. This liability (taxes on salaries paid) should also be recorded. The amount should be computed by applying the applicable rate to the appropriate wage base. Unlike the payroll tax accrual for unpaid salaries, the tax accrual for paid salaries should not be reversed. This is the amount that will actually be paid to the taxing authority for the period—payroll taxes become due on a cash rather than an accrual basis.

There are two significant types of fringe benefit expenses that should be recorded in special journals in order to reflect properly their cost and the associated liabilities within an organization's financial statements. These expenses involve an organization's obligation to make future payments to employees for vested rights to future time off and to pension funds for benefits earned by employees during an acounting period.

Financial Accounting Standards Board (FASB) Statement Number 43, Accounting for Compensated Absences, requires that organizations establish a liability by recording expenses associated with future time off earned by employees during an accounting period. The expense must be recorded only if four conditions exist. These conditions are:

- The liability to make future payments must relate to services performed by employees during an accounting period;
- The right to receive compensation is not contingent on future performance, that is, the rights are vested;
- It is reasonable to expect the amounts will actually be paid in the future; and
- The dollar value of the expense can be reasonably estimated.

Expenses that must be recorded pursuant to the requirements of FASB 43 usually involve vacations. If all of the above criteria are met, the following entry must be recorded each accounting period:

Debit Vacation Expense

Credit Fringe Benefits Payable.

When benefits are paid in a subsequent period, the disbursement is charged (debited) against the liability.

Expenses associated with future obligations payable for certain pension plans should be recorded in the period the obligations are incurred rather than when they are paid. This treatment is required by FASB Statement Number 87, Employers' Accounting for Pensions. A liability should be established that reflects unpaid amounts that will ultimately be due to a plan's trustee by recording the following entry:

Debit Pension Expense (Cost)

Credit Pension Costs Payable.

When contributions are made to the plan, the following entry is made to reduce the liability:

Debit Pension Costs Payable

Credit Cash.

Specific methods for computing current period pension expenses are addressed in FASB 87.

Summarizing Transactions

General Ledger. An organization's general ledger is a formal record of account balances. Transactions that are recorded in journals are posted monthly to the general ledger account that they impact. At the end of an accounting period the prior month's balance (as recorded in the general ledger) is adjusted to reflect the debits and credits posted from summary and special journals to arrive at the ending balance for the current month. Individual transactions lose their unique identity within the general ledger format. Therefore, it is important to provide for a tracking mechanism to identify an entry's source should retrospective review of activity affecting an account balance be necessary. Accordingly, each entry should be posted with an identifying reference. For instance, entries posted from the cash receipts and disbursements journals can be identified with the references C/R and C/D, respectively. Entries posted form payroll journals can be identified with the notation P/R. Special journals are usually identified numerically. Exhibit 6-2 illustrates a general ledger cash account.

As illustrated in Exhibit 6-2, the beginning cash balance of $1,000 was adjusted for cash receipts of $1,000, cash disbursements of $200, and payroll disbursements of $750, and a special journal entry (e.g., correcting entry) of $10 to arrive at the balance at 5/30/xx of $1,060. The ending balance at 5/30/xx becomes the beginning balance for the following month.

Balances in asset and liability accounts are carried forward perpetually. Revenue and expense balances are carried forward monthly; however, they are "closed-out" at the end of each year as a means of adjusting an organization's surplus account for the year's profit or loss. At year-end an entry is made to close or cancel out the balance of each revenue and expense account. The total debit amount necessary to close revenue acounts is posted to the income summary account as a credit; the total credit amount necessary to close expense accounts is posted as a debit to the income summary account. If the resulting balance in the income summary account is a credit, the organization realized a profit for the year. If the balance is a debit, a loss has been incurred. The balance in the income summary account is then closed through an entry to the surplus account. At the end of an organization's fiscal year, all revenue and expense accounts as well as the income summary should have a balance of zero.

Exhibit 6-2
General Ledger Cash Account

Date	Activity Debits	Activity Credits	Ref.	Balance Debit	Balance Credit
				$1,000	
5/30/xx	$1,000		C/R		
5/30/xx		$ 200	C/D		
5/30/xx		750	P/R		
5/30/xx	10		JE#1	1,060	

Trial Balance. Once all journals are posted to an organization's general ledger and account balances are updated to reflect the current period activity, a schedule of all accounts and their respective balances should be prepared. This schedule is referred to as trial balance. The trial balance serves two useful purposes. First, it functions as an accounting control. An imbalance condition would indicate an error in recording transactions in journals and/or an error in posting journals to the general ledger. Second, the trial balance is a useful tool in preparing financial statements.

Financial Statements. All organizations that rely upon financial support need to assess their financial condition periodically as impacted by the support received and expenses incurred. In for-profit, taxable entities sales activities generate revenues while manufacturing and selling/administration activities result in expenses. Revenues in excess of expenses enhance an organization's financial condition. Conversely, expenses in excess of revenues weaken an organization's financial condition. Although the underlying motivation in terms of operational objectives is somewhat different for tax-exempt, not-for-profit organizations, management and administrators must perceive their exempt organizations in terms of this "bottom-line" philosophy in order to ensure successfully the organization's continued existence and growth. The term nonprofit as used in conjunction with tax-exempt organizations is misleading. Put simply, nonprofit means that revenues in excess of expenses are retained within the organization (as opposed to being distributed to stockholders, owners, or partners) to enable the organization to continue serving in its tax-exempt capacity. Accordingly, not-for-profit, tax-exempt organizations measure operating performance and financial condition in much the same manner as do their taxable counterparts.

There are two basic financial reports that are used to measure the effectiveness of an organization's financial performance. In taxable organizations the reports are commonly a Statement of Financial Position or Balance Sheet, and a Profit and Loss Statement. The Profit and Loss Statement in most exempt organizations is commonly referred to as a Statement of Operations and Changes in Fund Balance. There is a third, less common, statement used by some exempt organizations. This statement is referred to as a Statement of Cash Flows.

An exempt organization's balance sheet depicts an organization's financial condition at a given point in time, that is, the close of the accounting period. The format for balance sheet presentation is somewhat standard for all organizations regardless of their tax status and/or organizational motivation (profit versus not-for-profit). The balance sheet consists of two broad classifications: assets, and liabilities and fund balance. The relationship between these classifications is the same relationship illustrated by the standard accounting equation discussed earlier in this chapter. Put succinctly, a balance sheet illustrates an organization's net worth (fund balance or surplus) in terms of its resources and obligations at a given point in time.

The asset section of the balance sheet consists of two broad subdivisions, current assets and other assets. Each subdivision is comprised of several line items reflecting homogeneous groupings of individual account balances. These groupings should be listed in order of liquidity in order for the presentation to conform with standard accepted reporting practices.

Current assets are cash and those assets that will be converted to cash or used within a twelve-month period. Cash and cash equivalents (commercial paper, certificates of deposit, and so on), receivables, materials/supplies, and prepaid expenses are examples of current assets.

The amount reported under the caption "cash and cash equivalents" is the combined total of all general ledger cash and short-term investment account balances. In some instances, organizations may wish to show short-term investments separately. This is a matter of individual preference based upon an organization's unique circumstances. As a general rule, investments having a maturity of three months or less can be treated as cash equivalents. Other investments should be shown separately. An organization's receivables do not need to, and should not, be grouped into one line item within the current asset section. Rather, the grouping of receivable accounts for balance sheet presentation should be reflective of an organization's base of financial support, the largest source being shown first. For example, organizations that rely heavily on federal grants and modestly on public pledges should show federal grants first. It should be noted that only that portion of grants and/or pledges which an organization expects to be realized within one year should be included within the current asset section; amounts due after one year should be shown under other assets. When combining receivable account balances for purposes of balance sheet presentation, the balances in the contra accounts (allowances for uncollectables) should be netted against the respective receivables. Miscellaneous receivables such as advances to employees should be grouped and presented under the balance sheet caption "other current assets."

Other current assets, such as supplies, prepaid expenses, and so on, can be grouped into one line item under the caption "other current assets," or they can be shown separately. The governing factor in determining the best method of presentation should be their relative materiality with respect to the organization's aggregate asset base.

Other (noncurrent) assets consist of items that are not expected to be converted to cash and/or will not lose their usefulness within one year. Examples include long-term investments (e.g., long-term corporate debt obligations), fixed assets and grants/pledges due after a one-year period. The order of presentation for noncurrent assets is also governed by relative liquidity. Long-term grants receivable are generally reported first, followed by investments, and property and equipment.

Long-term investments are usually reported in the amount of their historical cost; however, differences in cost and relative market value are sometimes reflected within the balance sheet. Long-term corporate debt obligations are carried and reported at their historical cost (adjusted for amortization of premiums or discounts). This treatment results in an asset balance equal to actual proceeds at the time of maturity. Equity investments (common stocks) are reflected within the balance sheet at the lower of cost or market value. This determination, however, is not made on an individual basis. The relative value of the total portfolio governs. If the aggregate market value of all common stocks is less than the aggregate cost, the lower market value is reported on the balance sheet by reducing the asset account balance by the balance in an offset account commonly called "reserve for security valuation." The security valuation reserve account reflects the cumulative amount of unrealized losses incurred in connection with an organization's common stock portfolio; unrealized losses, that is, entries impacting the security valuation reserve, are reflected within current period income determinations. Unrealized gains are not reflected on the balance sheet. Fixed assets are reported on the balance sheet in the amount of their net book value. Net book value is computed by netting asset balances with their accumulated depreciation accounts.

Liabilities are reported on the balance sheet in much the same manner as assets. The current liabilities section consists of current obligations (those that will be satisfied within a one-year period). The remaining liabilities (obligations payable after one year) are reported as other or noncurrent liabilities.

Current liabilities should be listed in a sequence that reflects their relative order of expected payment. The legal enforceability of the respective obligations should also be considered when determining the sequential placement of current liabilities. However, this should be a secondary consideration. Generally, current liabilities are presented in the following order: deferred revenue (income for future periods), accounts payable, and other current liabilities.

The other liability section of the balance sheet should include all long-term obligations, such as notes and bonds payable after one year. For purposes of presentation, the current portion of long-term debt balances should be reclassified and included within the current liability section.

Fund balances should be shown below liabilities on the balance sheet. In total, an organization's surplus or fund balance is the excess of assets over liabilities. For balance sheet presentation it is common to show multiple line items. The presentation should disclose, by line item identification, legal and/or other restricted funds, designated funds, and general contingency (unrestricted/undesignated) funds.

The exempt organization's counterpart to a profit and loss statement is referred to as a Statement of Operations and Changes in Fund Balance. The purpose of this statement is to summarize an organization's financial activity in terms of revenues over a specified period of time. In this regard, the statement of operations and changes in fund balance differs from the balance sheet; the former statement shows the results of current period activity while the latter depicts the impact of that activity on an organization's resources at the close of the accounting period.

As its purpose implies, the statement of operations and changes in fund balance has two major sections—revenues and expenses. The difference between total revenues and total expenses is added to (subtracted from) the fund balance at the beginning of the accounting period to arrive at the fund balance at the end of the accounting period. The fund balance at the end of the accounting period as shown on the statement of operations and changes in fund balance should agree with the fund balance shown on the statement of financial position.

Both the revenue and expense sections of the statement of operations and changes in fund balance consist of several line items. Generally, each line item represents a homogeneous grouping of similar accounts. Line items within each section should be listed in descending order of amount in order to depict their relative importance or impact on the organization's operation.

The statement of cash flows is a relative newcomer to financial reporting for both taxable and tax-exempt organizations. This statement is described within FASB Number 95 (Statement of Cash Flows). Although FASB 95 does not require not-for-profit organizations to present this statement, some not-for-profit organizations may find it useful to include a statement of cash flows in their reporting package.

The statement of cash flows depicts, by activity, an organization's sources and uses of cash. For purposes of this statement there are three types of activities that are presumed to generate or use cash. The statement shows cash flows (sources and use) from operating activities, investing activities, and financing activities.

The first section of the statement, cash flows from operating activities, begins with an organization's net profit or loss for the period. The specific line item, "excess of revenue over expense," or conversely "expenses in excess of revenues," is the initial point to begin computing the amount of cash provided (used) by operations. Since both the revenue and expense categories are impacted by a variety of entries involving noncash transactions (depreciation, amortization, rcognition of receivables and payables, and so on), the organization's "bottom line" must be purified to neutralize the effects of these transactions in order to determine accurately the actual cash provided by or used by operations. In order to accomplish this "neutralization" the following adjustments are necessary:

- Current period results are increased in the amount of noncash expense items (depreciation, amortization).
- Current period results are adjusted for other noncash transactions

that impacted the results. Specifically, current period results are decreased by increases in receivables and decreases in payables.

- Current period results are increased by decreases in receivables and increases in payables.

The result of applying these adjustments will be the net cash provided (or used) by operating activities.

The second section of the statement, cash flows from investing activities, summarizes certain cash transactions that did not directly impact current period income determinations. Cash flows from investing activities include purchases of property/equipment (decreases cash), sales of property/equipment (increases cash), purchases of investments (decreases cash), sales of investments (increases cash).

The third section of the statement, cash flows from financing activities, summarizes the impact that debt-related transactions have on an organization's cash reserves. Increases in an organization's short-term and/or long-term debt increase cash, while decreases in these liabilities decrease cash.

The aggregate increase or decrease in cash, as computed in the three sections of the statement of cash flows, is then applied to the cash balance at the beginning of the accounting period to arrive at the cash balance at the end of the accounting period. The latter balance should agree with the cash balance shown on the balance sheet.

while both the statement of cash flows and the statement of operations and changes in fund balance summarize activity, the perspective from which they do so differs. However, each statement is a valuable tool in measuring performance; thus, it is recommended that both statements be included in an organization's standard reporting package.

Exhibits 6-3, 6-4, and 6-5 illustrate each of the statements discussed within this section. As illustrated within the exhibits, data is presented for both the current and prior years. Comparative presentation of financial data provides statement users with a means of assessing financial condition and evaluating performance on an ongoing basis. Favorable and/or unfavorable trends are easily recognized. For purposes of fiscal planning, the timely detection of both favorable and unfavorable trends is essential.

SUMMARY

Not-for-profit, tax-exempt organizations are not unlike their for-profit, taxable counterparts with respect to their need for timely and accurate financial information. An organization needs a formal, systematic system for recording and summarizing financial transactions. Such a system must be designed in a manner that reflects the unique attributes of an organization both in terms of the organization's exempt functions and the environment in which the organization operates. An organization's accounting system should be complemented by a system of internal controls. Internal controls should not be organizationally isolated within the accounting function; rather they should exist throughout the organization and be considered an integral part of the organization's culture. The organization's system of internal controls should be communicated to employees at all levels, and the importance of the control environment should be stressed in employee publications and workshops.

Exhibit 6-3
Skyview Research Institute, Balance Sheet (December 31, 19xx and 19xy)

Assets	19xx	19xy
Current assets:		
Cash	$ 20,007	$ 14,580
Investments	780,000	192,000
Accounts receivable - grants	122,128	113,194
Accounts receivable - pledges	38,909	145,289
Total current assets	961,044	465,063
Furniture and equipment, at cost	210,642	146,485
Less accumulated depreciation	(51,278)	(25,752)
	159,364	120,733
Total assets	$1,120,408	$ 585,796
Liabilities and Fund Balance		
Current liabilities:		
Revenue for future periods	$ 101,185	$ 33,888
Accounts payable	93,288	134,998
Accrued payroll taxes and fringe benefits	17,746	17,777
Other current liabilities	-	680
Total current liabilities	212,229	187,343
Fund balance - unrestricted:		
Designated	16,614	18,058
Undesignated	891,565	380,395
Total fund balance	908,979	398,453
Total liabilities and fund balance	$1,120,408	$ 585,796

Exhibit 6-4
Skyview Research Institute, Statement of Operations and Changes in Fund Balance (December 31, 19xx and 19xy)

	19xx	19xy
Revenues:		
Contributions	$1,396,112	$1,297,582
Grants	54,764	142,846
Interest income	70,801	50,268
Total revenue	1,521,677	1,490,696
Operating expenses:		
Salaries	545,744	598,114
Payroll taxes and fringe benefits	40,839	144,839
Professional services	159,486	180,567
Cost of floor space	84,375	84,618
Depreciation - furniture and equipment	21,102	19,689
Amortization - leasehold improvements	-	57,383
Other operating expenses	160,405	145,849
Total expenses	1,011,951	1,280,659
Excess of revenues over expenses	509,726	210,037
Fund balance, beginning of year	398,453	188,416
Fund balance, end of year	$ 908,179	$ 398,453

Exhibit 6-5
Skyview Research Institute, Statement of Cash Flows (December 31, 19xx and 19xy)

	19xx	19xy
Cash flows from operating activities:		
Excess of revenues over expense	$ 509,726	$ 210,037
Adjustments excess of revenues over expense to net cash provided by operations:		
Depreciation and amortization	21,102	77,072
Decrease in accounts receivable	97,446	20,058
Increase in revenue for future periods	67,297	15,020
Decrease in accounts payable	(42,411)	(5,000)
Total adjustments	143,434	107,150
Net cash provided by operating activities	653,160	317,187
Cash flows from investing activities:		
Proceeds from sale of investments	31,470,000	30,580,000
Purchases of investments	(32,058,000)	(31,600,000)
Purchases of furniture and equipment	(59,733)	(20,650)
Net cash (used) in investing activities	(647,733)	(1,040,650)
Net increase (decrease) in cash	5,427	(723,463)
Cash balance at the beginning of year	14,580	738,043
Cash at the end of year	$ 20,007	$ 14,580

An organization's accounting system should embrace the concepts set forth within generally accepted accounting principles. The accrual method of accounting should be utilized as a means of ensuring the accumulation of meaningful financial data and enabling fiscal planning. Due professional care should be exercised in recording transactions, keeping in mind that the primary objective of financial accounting is to provide a meaningful matching of revenues and expenses.

Financial information should be periodically summarized in a standard reporting format. Financial reports should be designed to provide internal management and the general public with information concerning the financial condition of the organization as well as an indication of the organization's recent operating results. To enhance the meaningfulness of financial reports, comparative data from prior periods should be included within the reporting package.

Whenever practical, an organization should include financial information along with general communications to governmental units (regulatory bodies and funding agencies), private funding sources, members, employees, and the general public. An exempt organization's professionalism, integrity, and public commitment are directly reflected by financial disclosures to the public.

7

Financial Considerations: Practical Applications

INTRODUCTION

All tax-exempt organizations are responsible for performing activities pursuant to the basis of their exempt recognition. Management and/or administrators are responsible not only to the exempt organization's governing body but also to the public which the organization benefits. Public accountability is a paramount concern with far-reaching implications; management cannot take this responsibility lightly. Failure to maintain adequate levels of accountability can result in mismanagement, misappropriation of funds, loss of tax exemption, and in some cases, criminal prosecution.

Financial considerations play a major role in the effective management of an exempt organization. Exempt organizations are entrusted with funds earmarked for purposes deemed worthy of tax exemption. Management is responsible for safeguarding these funds and ensuring that the funds are used to further the purpose(s) set forth in the applicable Internal Revenue Code section governing the organization's tax exemption.

Prudent management of an exempt organization's financial resources requires a three-dimensional focus. The first and primary consideration involves the organization's internal control environment. In this regard, management is responsible for establishing and maintaining a system of internal controls sufficient to ensure that transactions are executed only in accordance with management's authorization, and that the transactions are recorded in the proper amount. The second area of focus involves prospective analysis and planning. An exempt organization's use of financial resources should be based upon a strategic plan developed in accordance with sound fiscal planning tools. Last, exempt organizations must review performance retrospectively. Retrospective review and analysis is necessary to identify areas requiring management attention and possible corrective action. Retrospective review of financial performance will enhance prospective planning efforts.

The purpose of this chapter is to provide a basic overview of internal control considerations and to present various methods of prospective planning techniques and retrospective review and analysis.

INTERNAL CONTROLS

The emphasis placed on the importance of an organization's system of internal controls has steadily increased since the mid-1970s. There have been several forces responsible for increasing public awareness of the importance of internal control systems. Unfortunately, these forces seem to come into play only after the discovery and disclosure of an aberrant situation. Even more disturbing is the fact that most current literature addressing the subject does so from the perspective of for-profit organizations, even though internal control concerns are equally important in nonprofit, tax-exempt organizations. Evidence of the importance of internal controls in tax-exempt organizations began surfacing in the latter half of the 1980s with the exposure of fraudulent activities involving certain television evangelists and the tax-exempt organizations that they advocated. Several of the abuses cited within news media coverage could have been prevented or detected earlier had the organizations adopted a sound system of internal controls.

One of the forces responsible for increased emphasis on internal controls was the enactment of the U.S. Foreign Corrupt Practices Act of 1977. While the primary focus of the act was to prohibit U.S. managers from bribing foreign officials to obtain business, the legislation requires managers to examine their organization's system of internal controls (with respect to illegal activities) and to implement corrective actions if material weaknesses are found to exist. Although the Foreign Corrupt Practices Act, an amendment to the Securities and

Exchange Act of 1934, applies only to organizations whose securities are publicly traded, many nonprofit, tax-exempt organizations have voluntarily taken positive steps to comply with the spirit of the act.

The concept of internal control must be perceived globally. Although internal controls, or the lack thereof, manifest themselves directly in the financial recording and reporting process, the controls themselves, in order to be effective, must transgress the organizational boundaries of financial functions. An effective system of internal controls should be embraced as part of an organization's culture. In this regard, the internal environment of the exempt organization must be maintained in a manner that promotes a constant awareness of the importance of internal controls. Ideally, the foundation of the control environment should be established at the time an organization is created, and management's intent with respect to maintaining the environment should be periodically communicated throughout the organization as a means of reinforcing the concepts and values implied by the very existence of a control system. The preceding statement is not intended to imply that the creation and maintenance of an internal control sytstem will preclude the occurrence of problems. Management and administrators should recognize that errors and irregularities (see Chapter 6) will necessarily occur because of the imperfections inherent in human nature; internal controls are intended only to minimize the number of such occurrences and to provide a mechanism of prudent prevention and early detection.

The recognition that no system of internal controls will guarantee the total absence of undesirable acts is an important consideration in the initial design of an organization's system of internal controls. Unrealistic expectations with respect to internal controls can lead to an overly strict environment and result in administrative inefficiencies. In this regard, an overly aggressive posture can ultimately paralyze an organization. In formulating an organization's control objectives, a delicate balance should be maintained. Risks should be assessed in terms of their relative impact to an organization's financial stability. Other variables impacting the risk assessment process include the size of the organization, the caliber of its employees, government regulations, the nature of the product or service provided, and the existence or lack thereof of oversight mechanisms external to the organization.

The subject of internal controls, the related disciplines, and the conceptual framework of their purpose and application have evolved over a number of years. The evolutionary process has been driven by standards developed and promulgated by several professional organizations. Both the American Institute of Certified Public Accountants (AICPA) and the Institute of Internal Auditors (IIA) have addressed internal control concerns in their professional standards. These standards are an excellent reference for the exempt organization desiring to establish a system of internal controls or to evaluate the effectiveness of an existing system.

While both certified public accountants and internal auditors are interested in internal controls, their respective concerns differ. Generally, certified public accountants examine controls governing the flow of financial information so that the controls can be relied upon for audit testing and for expressing an opinion on the organization's financial statements. The concern of internal auditors with respect to internal controls is somewhat broader. Internal auditors examine finance-related controls as well as controls governing various administrative processes.

Establishing an effective system of internal controls requires an objective assessment of the total organization. It is recommended that a two-tiered approach be adopted. First, the organization should be examined in the broadest possible context. It is from this perspective that global control objectives should be developed. Once the global objectives are identified, the organization should be reexamined in terms of its specific operations and functions. Specific objectives can then be tailored to the organization's unique operations. The control objectives should then be operationalized by being incorporated into formal policies and procedures.

Internal Controls—The Global Perspective

Global control objectives encompass the organization itself as well as environmental factors affecting the organization. In establishing control objectives relating to the organization proper, traditional delineations of function authority can be used to provide a basic framework. Broad objectives addressing wide areas of responsibility such as personnel administration, finance, public relations, operations, purchasing, and marketing or fund-raising can be defined in terms of each area's basic mission in a manner consistent with the organization's overall exempt purpose. Defining control objectives in terms of an organization's external environment is a more complex process inasmuch as there is no standard framework available with which to structure the necessary determinations. To facilitate the process it is suggested that the legal basis of an organization's tax-exempt recognition be used as a starting point.

Internal Controls—Functional Considerations

There are several ways to develop specific internal control objectives. The simplest method is to view the organization in terms of its basic operations: both the transactions arising from them, and the support functions necessary to maintain them. In its purest form, this approach ensures that virtually all areas of an organization are considered in the developmental stage of defining specific internal control objectives.

Operationalizing International Control Objectives

In order to be effective, internal control objectives need to be operationalized by identifying the specific processes and procedures necessary to accomplish their intended purpose. In developing specific control procedures, it is useful to consider some generic definitions relating to various types of controls. It should be noted that these definitions are not always mutually exclusive; specific control procedures can, and often do, fall under one or more of the following categories:

Accounting Controls. The term accounting control relates to specific procedures designed to ensure that all financial transactions are recorded, recorded in the proper amount, and reported properly on an organization's financial statements. Accounting controls also encompass procedures considered necessary to ensure that an organization's assets are appropriately safeguarded. Accounting controls relate exclusively to matters directly affecting an organization's financial statements. Examples of accounting controls include routine checks and balances over daily cash receipts, separation of duties within various accounting functions, and required management authorization of financial commitments.

Administrative Controls. Administrative controls involve internal procedures relating to operational and administrative efficiencies. Administrative controls relate to matters having an indirect impact on an organization's financial statements. Examples of administrative controls include quality studies, budget preparation and review processes, employee hiring practices, training and development programs, and compensation procedures and strategies.

Detective Controls. As the name implies, detective controls are those procedures designed to detect errors and irregularities. Detective controls almost always involve financial matters, thus they relate closely to accounting controls. The relationship between accounting controls and detective controls is that the latter can be considered a subset of the former. Another way of describing the relationship is to state that while most detective controls are accounting controls, not all accounting controls are detective controls. Examples of detective controls include general ledger account analysis, bank statement reconciliations, physical inventories of materials and supplies, and testing of general ledger account balances.

Preventive Controls. Preventive controls are those procedures designed to prevent errors or irregularities from occurring in the first place. In terms of both strength and desirability, preventive controls are considered superior to detective controls. Inasmuch as preventive controls normally relate to errors and irregularities involving financial matters, they can also be considered a subset of accounting controls. Examples of preventive controls include payroll balancing routines, input/output checks, and functional separation of duties.

Population Controls. Population controls are those specific controls designed to ensure that all financial information is entered into and processed through the accounting system. Population controls safeguard the organization against unrecorded transactions; hence, they contribute to the overall integrity of an organization's financial data and accountability over an organization's assets. Population controls can either be preventive or detective in nature.

Accuracy Controls. Accuracy controls work in conjunction with population controls. The purpose of accuracy controls is to ensure that the information entered into the accounting system is recorded in the proper amount. The interplay between population controls and accuracy controls can be illustrated by examining an order entry process using prenumbered sales order forms as population control. A manual and/or automated check to establish that all sales orders are accounted for ensures only that all sales orders are entered into the system. While this population control ensures the capture of data for subsequent billing, it does not ensure the integrity of that data. Accuracy controls such as checking pricing extensions are necessary to ensure the sales are billed in the proper amount.

Internal Controls and Tax Compliance

When establishing a system of internal controls in a tax-exempt organization, tax compliance issues cannot be ignored. In this regard, there are many diverse considerations. The diversity is attributable not only to the numerous types of exemptions recognized by the Internal Revenue Code but also to numerous restrictions unique to each particular type of exempt organization. While a "laundry list" of all internal control concerns unique to tax-exempt organizations is beyond the scope of this text, a list of the major concerns may prove useful to exempt organizations' financial managers in assessing their particular environment. The following discussions address some of the more common internal control concerns unique to exempt organizations. The information contained in the following paragraphs, particularly the recommended control procedures, is presented from a general overview perspective. It is suggested that the recommended control procedures be analyzed in terms of their particular applicability to a specific organization's policies and procedures. Additionally, it is suggested that financial managers review the IRS regulations applicable to their particular organization and develop a more specific listing.

Private Inurement. Several types of tax-exempt organizations are prohibited from permitting any part of their net earnings to inure to the benefit of private shareholders and/or individuals. Private inurement restrictions apply to several exempt organizations, including those described within Internal Revenue Code Sections 501(c)(3), 501(c)(4), 501(c)(6), 501(c)(9), 501(c)(11), and 501(c)(13). The basic control objective applicable to these organizations is to avoid transactions involving private inurement. Inadvertent acts involving private inurement should be readily identifiable. Controls should be in place to ensure timely correction of such acts. Some of the controls that an organization can install to accomplish the preceding objectives involve both accounting and administrative considerations. The policy manual of the organization should expressly prohibit employees, officers, and directors from engaging in any act involving private inurement. Procedures should be sufficiently detailed to as to provide for review of questionable transactions prior to their execution; the approval process should be relied upon to prompt review at appropriate management levels.

Transactions Jeopardizing Exempt Recognition. Tax-exempt organizations are recognized as such because their basic mission is to carry on one or more of the tax-exempt purposes described within the Internal Revenue Code Section applicable to their exempt purpose. Material deviations from an organization's recognized tax-exempt purpose will result in the loss of tax-exempt recognition. Material deviations more often than not manifest themselves in the transactions with which an organization involves itself. Hence, the control objective that all exempt organizations should adopt is to avoid material transactions (either on an individual and/or aggregate basis) that jeopardize an organization's tax-exempt recognition. Both accounting and administrative controls can be installed to accomplish this objective. An organization's training and development program should include training sessions educating employees in matters involving the basis of an organization's tax exemption; training sessions should be designed to emphasize the negative consequences of particular types of activities. Written guidelines discussing the basis of an organization's tax exemption and the organization's primary mission should be provided to all employees. Accounting procedures should require special management approval for all transactions not expressloy covered by the organization's mission statement. Consideration should be given to organizing a special committee, comprised of management and outside directors, charged with the responsibility of reviewing nonroutine transactions.

Restrictions on Lobbying. Organizations described in Internal Revenue Code Section 501(c)(3) are prohibited from substantially engaging in activities relating to carrying on propaganda or otherwise attempting to influence legislation, and from attempting to participate or intervene in any political campaign. The control objective here is obvious—to avoid prohibited activities as they relate to propaganda, influencing legislation, and/or political campaigns. The control procedures are similar to those relating to avoiding transactions that jeopardize an organization's exempt purpose. Administrative controls involving training and development programs addressing the restrictions on lobbying are probably the best preventive measure. In addition, accounting procedures should require that all expenditures involving transactions that appear politically motivated be reviewed and approved, at appropriate management levels, prior to the time that expenditures are made. Management reports, summarizing all expenditures made to advocate particular causes and/or public issues, should be periodically prepared and reviewed at appropriate management levels.

Unrelated Business Taxable Income. Under certain circumstances, tax-exempt organizations are subject to tax, at regular corporate tax rates, on income earned from activities unrelated to their recognized exempt purpose. To be considered taxable, three criteria must be met. The income must be earned in connection with an activity considered to be a trade or business; the trade or business must be conducted on a regular basis; and the trade or business must be substantially unrelated to the organization's tax-exempt purpose. In some respects, the control objectives relating to unrelated business income and the tax imposed thereon are similar to the concerns involving transactions jeopardizing an organization's tax exemption. Yet, in other ways, the control concerns are different. Controls should ensure that earnings derived from activities determined to be unrelated are not permitted to overshadow, in terms of relative financial significance, income realized from the performance of tax-exempt activities. In this regard, training sessions and written guidelines addressing the nature and extent of permitted/prohibited activities should be a mandatory part of an organization's training and development program. Reports detailing the relative significance of unrelated business income should be prepared and reviewed by management on a regular basis. The organization's accounting system should be designed in a manner that permits the identification of unrelated revenues and the expenses associated with these revenues for subsequent reporting to the IRS. Controls should ensure that all expenses associated with unrelated revenues (including overhead allocations) are captured in order to minimize the organization's tax burden.

Private Foundations. Exempt organizations described in Internal Revenue Code Section 501(c)(3) that are deemed to be private foundations (see Chapter 5) have a significantly greater need for internal controls than do other tax-exempt organizations. Private foundations are subject to several unique restrictions, reporting requirements, and excise taxes. Private foundations are not permitted to engage in certain transactions with substantial contributors and other disqualified parties. Private foundations are subject to a 2 percent excise tax on their net investment income, and are limited with respect to their investment options. Restrictions exist limiting private ownership in unrelated business enterprises as well as other investments jeopardizing a foundation's exempt purpose. Additionally, private foundations are required to maintain a minimum level of charitable expenditures annually. Failure to comply with any and/or all of these restrictions will result in the imposition of excise (penalty) taxes; excise taxes are imposed on a "tiered" basis increasing to a maximum of 100 percent in cases of repeated or willful disregard. Repeated and/or willful violations can also result in the foundation being involuntarily terminated by the IRS. The control objectives of a private foundation should address these restrictions from both an administrative and accounting perspective; due to the severity of noncompliance penalties, it is imperative that control procedures relating to the various objectives be, to the fullest extent possible, preventive rather than detective in nature. Additionally, control procedures should be as specific as possible to prevent instances of misunderstanding and unintentional violations.

To address the compliance issues discussed in the preceding paragraph, a private foundation should develop accounting and administrative procedures necessary to accomplish the following objectives:

- Transactions involving substantial contributors or other disqualified persons should be entered into only after appropriate reviews are conducted to determine whether or not the transactions constitute prohibited acts of self-dealing as described in Internal Revenue Code Section 4941. Transactions determined to constitute prohibited acts of self-dealing should be avoided or restructured;
- Equity investments in unrelated businesses that involve the foundation's funds should be closely scrutinized to ensure that established limits of control (with respect to business ownership and co-participation of disqualified persons and/or other parties) are not exceeded;
- Investment strategies should ensure that the foundation's funds are not utilized in a manner that jeopardizes the foundation's exempt purpose; and
- Charitable expenditures should be made in sufficient amounts so as to ensure that statutory floors are met.

There are several policies and procedures that can be utilized to accomplish the control objectives discussed in the preceding paragraph. The following suggestions can, and probably should, be expanded to facilitate their implementation in specific organizations.

The legal definitions of substantial contributors and other disqualified persons should be included in the organization's policy and procedures manual. Understandable interpretations should also be included. Likewise, discussions with respect to prohibited transactions should be addressed in the policy and procedures manual. Monthly reports summarizing all transactions with substantial contributors and other disqualified persons (regardless of whether they involve self-dealing) should be prepared by each responsibility center; these reports should be submitted to a designated management representative for review and analysis to determine whether inadvertent and/or other acts of self-dealing occurred. Transactions that are identified as prohibited acts of self-dealing should be corrected immediately. A list of all substantial contributors and other disqualified persons should be maintained. This listing should be kept current by updating it on a monthly basis. Updated lists should be distributed to appropriate management and staff personnel. All transactions involving substantial contributors and other disqualified persons should be subject to a special management approval process; approvals should be withheld for any transaction resembling a prohibited act. Procedures should require that questionable transactions be referred to legal counsel for review and functional approval prior to their execution.

Formal investment guidelines should be established. These guidelines should address the various legal restrictions applicable to the foundation's investments. The foundation's board of directors or other governing body should establish an investment committee. This committee should be given oversight responsibility with respect tothe foundation's investment stratgegies and the composition of the foundation's investment portfolio. Investment transactions should be subject to a special approval process, a process separate and distinct from the approval process governing other purchasing and sales activities.

Due diligence should be exercised to ensure that adequate levels of the foundation's expenditures meet the appropriate criteria of qualifying distributions set forth within Internal Revenue Code Section 4942. To accomplish the underlying control objective, that is, to meet statutory floors with respect to charitable expenditures, it is necessary to establish a formal policy specifying what types of expenditure fall within permitted categories. Expenditures that are not included within permitted categories should be subjected to a well-defined review and approval process. Procedures should be established to monitor effectively relative levels of charitable and noncharitable expenditures. In this regard, specific accounting procedures should be designed to segregate qualifying amounts form nonqualifying amounts. The underlying accounting records should be maintained in a manner that identifies not only current levels but also prior levels of qualifying versus nonqualifying expenditures in order to ensure the capture and application of any carryover amounts. Periodic reports summarizing relative expenditure activity should be prepared and submitted to the foundation's senior management and governing body to ensure prompt corrective action if such action is necessary.

The Transaction Cycle Approach

Many public accounting firms and internal audit organizations have adopted what has become known as the "transaction cycle" approach to evaluating internal controls. Although this approach was originally conceptualized as a method of evaluating internal controls, it can also be used as an effective tool in establishing a system of internal controls. Its generic framework facilitates its application in any organization regardless of tax status.

The cycle approach, as it applies to establishing a system of internal controls, requires three fundamental tasks. First, an organization's basic transaction cycles must be identified. The identification process should include isolating all of the organization's activities relating to the various transaction cycles. The second phase of the approach is to establish criteria defining desired performance and/or expected results. Standards of desired performance and expected results are the actual control objectives of the organization. The third phase is probably the most difficult. This phase involves developing policies and procedures necessary to accomplish the control objectives of each transaction cycle.

Transaction Cycles. Transaction cycles may vary from organization to organization. Although there is a degree of variance, most exempt organizations should be able to relate their respective operations to the following transaction cycles:

- Revenues and receipts;
- Expenses, disbursements, and payables;
- Investments and cash flow;
- Capital expenditures and fixed assets; and
- Payroll and personnel administration.

It is important to note that the above transaction cycles transgress typical organizational lines of authority and responsibility. Defining transaction cycles in this manner facilitates the design and implementation of a fully integrated system of internal controls. Global integration is necessary to minimize instances of control failure that can result from fragmented procedures unique to individual operating units within the organization. Clear objectives in terms of the total transaction cycle will ensure that one operating unit does not overlook considerations under a false assumption that other operating units are responsible for accomplishing certain control objectives.

Establishing Criteria. Establishing criteria for desired results, that is, control objectives, requires a logical examination of the substances of the organization's fiscal activity rather than specific transactions. For instance, an organization having several sources of revenue (such as federal grants, general public contributions, and income from the performance of services) will probably have the same concerns about revenue regardless of its source. In other words, control objectives should be broad enough to encompass all possible transactions within a transaction cycle. Establishing narrow objectives within transaction cycles can lead to overlooked concerns and result in inadequate and/or incomplete procedures. Although control objectives will vary from organization to organization, there are several basic objectives that apply to all organizations. Exhibit 7-1 illustrates a number of control objectives within each of the five transaction cycles. Exhibit 7-1 does not contain all possible control objectives; organizations should expand this information to fit their unique circumstances.

Control Procedures. After transaction cycles are identified and control objectives are established, specific procedures necessary to accomplish the objectives must be developed and implemented. There is an infinite number of control procedures that can be employed by an organization. The following paragraphs discuss a number of these procedures. It is important to note that while one procedure can be employed to accomplish several objectives, it may be necessary to employ several procedures to accomplish one objective. An organization's specific attributes should be the governing factor with respect to the number and type of controls selected.

An organization's structure can be employed as a control if it is designed in a manner that provides for a degree of separation of duties. Proper segregation of duties with respect to both broad departmental responsibility assignments and intradepartmental workflows will result in a workable system of checks and balances. For example, unauthorized disbursements can be prevented and/or detected by separating the responsibilities of the purchasing department from those of the accounting and treasury departments. Using this structure, no one area can control all aspects of a transaction. Unauthorized purchase commitments made within the purchasing area would be detected in the accounts payable unit of the accounting department assuming the existence of authorization requirements. Similarly, unauthorized checks issued by the treasury department would be detected within the accounting area assuming that the accounting area is responsible for reconciling monthly disbursements generated in its area with independent control totals extracted from the actual payment checks. The accounting area, not having custody of payment checks, is prevented from issuing an unauthorized check. Controls are enhanced by separating the duties within each of these three departments. For example, a balancing routine whereby the output of an accounts payable system is balanced to a control total developed by an employee other than the employee responsible for inputting data to the system would detect incorrect and/or unauthorized payments.

Exhibit 7-1
Transaction Cycles

Cycle: Revenues and Receipts

Control Objectives:

1. Funds requested for a specific project should be requested in amounts sufficient to cover the cost associated with conducting the project.

2. Proposals for the performance of services should contain all necessary pricing data; prices should be established based upon sound financial review and analysis.

3. Specific grant budgets, project proposals and pricing literature should be properly authorized.

4. All amounts due should be invoiced and/or requested on a timely basis; controls should ensure that this is done, and that all requests and invoices are in the proper amount.

5. Prices should be appropriately authorized; discounts and/or special pricing arrangement made on an exception basis should be subject to a specific review and approval process.

Exhibit 7-1 (continued)

6. Accounts receivable should be monitored and procedures should be installed to ensure timely identification of delinquent amounts.

7. Revenues, regardless of source and type, should be recorded within the general ledger accounts when earned; receivables should be recorded at the time of revenue recognition.

8. Cash receipts should be properly applied and be deposited on a timely basis.

Cycle: Expenses, Disbursements and Payables

Control Objectives:

1. Commitments requiring the expenditure of funds should be subjected to a formal review and approval process.

2. Cash disbursements should be made only for approved commitments.

3. Unsigned payment checks should be appropriately safeguarded.

4. Authority to sign disbursement checks should be restricted to a limited number of management personnel. Unless it is impractical, two signatures should be required on all disbursement checks.

5. Disbursements should be made only after authorizations are received and supporting documentation is reviewed to ascertain the correctness of amounts billed.

6. Signature plates should be appropriately safeguarded.

7. All unpaid amounts due to third parties should be properly reflected as payables in the general ledger accounts; expenses should be recorded when incurred rather than when paid.

8. Payments should be made on a timely basis and in the proper amount; early payment discounts should be taken when possible.

9. Vendor criteria should be established; purchase commitments should be made only with designated vendors.

Cycle: Investments and Cash Flow

Control Objectives:

1. Uncommitted funds should be invested in interest bearing instruments to the fullest extent possible.

2. Investment criteria should be developed that limit discretionary placements to securities of a specified grade.

3. Investment securities should be appropriately safeguarded.

4. Investment commitments should be made by a limited number of designated management personnel.

5. All bank accounts should be reconciled on a regular basis.

Exhibit 7-1 (continued)

6. Petty cash funds should be appropriately safeguarded; access should be limited to designated fund custodians.

7. Investment transactions should be properly accounted for; balances should be reflected in the general ledger accounts in the manner prescribed by generally accepted accounting principles.

Cycle: Capital Expenditures and Fixed Assets

Control Objectives:

1. Commitments for the acquisition of fixed assets and other capital expenditures should be subjected to a review and approval process that is separate and distinct from the process governing other disbursements.

2. Capital acquisitions should be accounted for in designated fixed asset accounts.

3. A formal depreciation/amortization policy should be developed; expense entries should be based upon a detailed fixed asset register and depreciation schedule.

4. Fixed assets should be appropriately safeguarded.

5. Periodic physical inventories of fixed assets should be conducted; discrepancies between the results of the inventory and general ledger account balances should be investigated and resolved on a timely basis.

6. Sales and/or other transactions resulting in the transfer of title to fixed assets should be approved at appropriate management levels.

7. Assets pledged as collateral in financing arrangements should be identified in a formal document and appropriate restrictions should be imposed preventing inadvertent sale and/or title transfers.

Cycle: Payroll and Personnel

Control Objectives:

1. Position applicants should be screened to confirm qualifications and experience.

2. Employees should be placed on the payroll only after specified approvals are made.

3. Wage and salary payments should be made only to bona fide employees.

4. Equal opportunity and/or affirmative action policies should be developed and communicated to all employees. Compliance mechanisms should be established; compliance should be monitored on a periodic basis.

5. Wage and salary guidelines should be established. Wage and salary payments should conform to these guidelines.

Exhibit 7-1 (continued)

6. Wages and salaries should be properly reflected in the general ledger accounts; provisions should be made to recognize expenses associated with unpaid salary/wage liabilities at the close of an accounting period.

7. Payroll taxes and other withholding liabilities should be properly accounted for and the amounts withheld should be paid on a timely basis.

8. Employers' payroll tax expense should be computed in the prescribed manner and liabilities should be satisfied on a timely basis.

9. Payroll tax returns should be reviewed and signed by an appropriate official.

Segregation of duties can also be used in nonaccounting areas. For instance, the placement of a fictitious employee on the payroll can be prevented and/or detected by separating the employment function from the payroll function, assuming of course that new hires are approved at appropriate levels within the employment area. Periodic reconciliations should be conducted between the number of employees contained in staffing records and the corresponding number of payroll records; these reconciliations would serve as a detective control if a payroll clerk were to act unilaterally to add a fictitious employee.

Balancing routines are used extensively as a means of achieving several objectives of internal control. Control totals can be used by one employee to check his or her own work, or by several employees in conjunction with one another. A bank reconciliation is one form of a balancing routine; the cash balance computed within the organization's accounting systems is "balanced" to an independent figure computed by the bank. An imbalance situation indicates (detects) either an internal error (within the accounting system) which would impact the integrity of the organization's financial statements or an error committed by the bank, which would have a direct impact on the organization's assets.

Control procedures are not limited to procedures commonly referred to as checks and balances. Control procedures can manifest themselves in the layout and design of an organization's place of business. These types of controls are referred to as physical controls. The primary objective of physical controls is to safeguard an organization's assets. Examples of physical controls include fireproof filing cabinets, restricted access areas, guard stations, fire and burglar alarms, safes, and surveillance cameras. While the primary objective of physical controls is to safeguard assets, there is a related benefit—employee safety.

Organizations that have electronic data-processing facilities have a unique set of concerns when evaluating the number and type of controls to install. Due to the heavy capital investment associated with computer equipment, physical controls are extremely important. In addition to physical controls, organizations that rely heavily on data processing must consider controls to ensure the integrity of the data processed by automated systems. Some of the more common controls include keystroke verification, validity (edit) checks, and readback capabilities. Keystroke verification is a technique used in an organization's data preparation unit. One employee rekeys the information previously keyed by another employee to ensure that the correct information is entered into the system. While this technique is a strong preventive control, it can be costly. Most organizations choose to limit verification activities to critical applications. A validity (edit) check is a technique employed within an automated system that tests the elements within a given input field for conformity with predetermined criteria such as a table of acceptable codes or values. Transactions failing predetermined edit checks are not accepted by the system; rather they are automatically referred back to the initiator of the input data for investigation and resolution. Readback is a procedure used in connection with a data input/display terminal. The individual inputting the data to an automated terminal can visually determine whether the system has accepted or rejected the data and/or ascertain whether further actions are necessary.

The design of all control procedures should be sufficient to accomplish the associated objectives; however, care should be taken not to "overcontrol" at the expense of productivity. Too many controls can be just as bad as no controls at all. In summary, it should be noted that internal control systems are the responsibility of an organization's management. A common misconception is that auditors are responsible for control systems. Both public accountants and internal auditors evaluate controls to accomplish their specific audit objectives. While they can rely on the adequacy controls to limit their testing and/or recommend additional control procedures, they are not responsible for installing and/or maintaining an organization's system of internal controls. Controls are a management responsibility.

PROSPECTIVE PLANNING

Sound fiscal planning (budgeting) is necessary to ensure the financial stability of any organization regardless of the organization's profit motivation and/or tax status. In the context of these discussions, the terms budgeting and financial/fiscal planning are synonymous; hence, they are used interchangeably. The absence of short- and long-term goals, in terms of both qualitative and quantitative elements, can result in operational inefficiencies and unfavorable financial results. Conversely, sound fiscal plans will enhance the probability of an organization's success. An organization's operating plan is necessarily related to its existing financial position and anticipated cash flow in both the short and long term. While there is always a degree of uncertainty in prospective financial analysis, the impact of that uncertainty can be minimized through prudent examination of an organization's internal and external environment. Environmental factors influencing the budgeting process include, but are not limited to, the availability of funds from external sources, anticipated price level changes, the composition of an organization's workforce, legislative considerations, and management philosophy. These factors should be systematically examined at the onset of each budget cycle and be reexamined at periodic intervals within the budget period.

Generally, there are two types of budgets to consider: operating budgets and capital budgets. In terms of relative complexity, operating budgets are more difficult to prepare. The difficulty stems from uncertainties related to identifying expected revenue sources necessary to support projected expenditures. Ironically, the impact of unfavorable budget deviations is more severe with respect to operating budgets. While it is relatively easy to defer capital expenditures if expected cash flows do not materialize, it is more difficult to control employment costs and other variable expenses in periods of cash shortfalls.

Operating Budgets

Operating budgets are normally prepared at two levels. Prior to the beginning of an organization's fiscal year, a global or consolidated budget, reflecting total expected receipts and associated expenses, should be prepared. This budget becomes the basis for measuring performance and initiating corrective actions if they are necessary. During the course of a fiscal period, it may be necessary to prepare project-specific budgets for submission to various funding agencies. Project-specific budgets and consolidated budgets are not mutually exclusive. Project-specific budgets, even though they may not apply to the fiscal period in which they are prepared, form the basis of the consolidated budget for the following fiscal period.

Revenues. The first factor to consider when preparing a consolidated budget is anticipated revenues. When forecasting revenues, a number of variables can be considered to minimize the degree of uncertainty, which, however, can never be completely eliminated. It is recommended that revenue projections be made on a conservative basis. Due to the numerous types of tax-exempt organizations, there is no "laundry list" of all factors to consider when projecting revenues; however, some of the more common elements are as follows:

- Pending grant applications being considered by funding agencies;
- Current trends in sales and/or contributions evidenced by historical financial results;
- Population changes;
- Legislative initiatives with respect to funding particular types of activities;
- The number and type of fund-raising activities planned by other tax-exempt organizations within the community; and
- General economic trends, indices, and other statistical data.

Larger organizations may wish to incorporate a degree of contingency planning in the process of forecasting revenues. This practice is particularly useful for organizations that rely on grants as their main revenue source. Expected cash flows from funding agencies can be forecasted under the assumption that if one agency rejects a grant application, another agency will consider funding the project in a different amount. It is in this regard that several tax-exempt organizations project revenues at three levels: pessimistic, optimistic, and most probable.

The forecasting of revenue is probably the most critical phase of the budgeting process. Revenue projections, like any goal, should be both reasonable and attainable.

Revenue related to project-specific budgets is relatively easy to forecast. Generally, public and private funding agencies that solicit project proposals disclose the award amount that they are considering. Since project grants are normally awarded on a cost reimbursement basis, the revenue associated with the project will be equal to the cost of performing the necessary tasks. Project costs can be easily computed using projected manpower allocations from the specific workplan. Employment costs (salaries and payroll taxes/fringes) generally comprise the major portion of a project's expense. Salary expense is merely an extension of planned hours adjusted for expected increases. Payroll taxes and fringes can be estimated based upon the historical ratio of the applicable expenses to total salary costs. For purposes of computing this ratio, both the numerator (payroll taxes and fringes) and the denominator (salary expense) should include data for several months, preferably one year.

Other costs associated with specific project proposals can be divided into three categories: allocations, project-specific expenses, and indirect costs. Allocations are defined as those costs that are directly related to expended effort. Examples include supplies and cost of floor space. Historical cost-per-hour data (adjusted for expected price level changes) can be used as a basis for projecting the cost allocations of a specific project. Project-specific expenses are costs directly attributable to the project. Examples of project-specific expenses include travel, subcontractor fees, and final report preparation expenses. Indirect costs are defined as overhead expenses incidental to, but not necessarily related to, the specific project. Examples of indirect costs are financial reporting and recordkeeping expenses. Indirect costs are normally computed using a standard indirect cost rate reflecting aggregate indirect costs as a percentage of aggregate direct expenses. Most federal agencies require recipient organizations to submit annual indirect cost proposals for purposes of establishing a standard rate of reimbursement for these costs.

Estimating revenues on a project-specific basis is nothing more than a basic pricing strategy. The accuracy and completeness of each proposal has a direct bearing on whether or not an organization will recover the costs associated with the project. Inaccurate and/or incomplete proposals can result in the organization's incurring a direct, measurable financial loss for a particular project.

Expenses. There are two generally accepted methodologies related to the preparation of expense budgets. The first methodology is known as zero-base budgeting. The second method is sometimes referred to as existing resource appropriation. The difference between these two methods involves an assumption relating to the base from which expense projections are made. The zero-base budgeting concept assumes that there are no existing employees and/or other expense commitments. Manpower needs and other administrative expenses are projected solely on the basis of the organization's operating plan. The existing resource appropriation method assumes the existence of a defined employee base; operating plans are formulated and the related expenses are projected within the constraints of the existing workforce and proposed additions thereto. Notwithstanding the practical difficulties related to the potential for erratic shifts in employment and other costs, zero-base budgeting is preferable to existing resource appropriation. Implementation of the zero-base methodology enhances an organization's ability to focus on only those projects necessary to accomplish its stated exempt purpose. Nonessential projects can be identified prior to making irreversible commitments.

Regardless of the method chosen, expense projections contained within operating expense budgets should be based upon reliable financial data in order to ensure that they are reasonable and attainable. In all but a few instances it is necessary to rely on historical cost information as a starting point. The reliance upon historical data, although it appears to be in conflict with the underlying objectives of zero-based budgeting, is not inconsistent with this approach. The starting point for zero-based budgeting is the organization's operating plan; assigning cost factors to this plan necessarily requires the use of a reasonable basis for estimating expenses.

The expense section of the organization's chart of general ledger accounts is the reference point from which to begin estimating expenses. Use of this document as a starting point minimizes the risk of overlooking specific expense categories. It should be recognized, however, that while using the chart of accounts minimizes the risk of inadvertent exclusion, new and/or unusual expense categories can arise in the budgeting process.

In service organizations, salary and wage expenses and payroll tax and fringe benefit costs normally amount to between 40 and 60 percent of total expenses. The relative impact of these expenses to exempt organizations that produce and/or sell products is somewhat less; however, the impact is still material to the overall expense base. When estimating salaries and wages, one should use the organization's operating plan as the primary reference point. In zero-base budgeting, the relative size of the workforce is governed by the workplan. When using other than zero-base budgeting models, the size of the workforce is still the primary reference point even though the assumption regarding relative size may be based upon a different set of variables.

Salary and wage projections should be based upon individual computations to the fullest extent possible. Contractual commitments with respect to scheduled increases and/or discretionary merit increases should be factored into the calculation. Particular attention should be given to anticipated collective bargaining settlements with respect to levels of pay. The likelihood of settlements at various levels should be analyzed and the most probable outcome should be used to project the expense.

Payroll taxes and fringe benefit expenses normally follow a consistent pattern in terms of their relationship with salaries and wages. Generally, the combined expense can be estimated as a percentage of salaries and wages based upon historical experience. It may be necessary to temper this estimate to account for certain benefit costs that vary significantly from year to year and/or that increase at a more rapid rate than salaries and wages. Particular attention should be given to the cost of health-care benefits. Historically, cost increases in this area have outpaced inflation; this expense can also vary significantly from one year to the next.

As a general rule, other administrative expenses can be estimated on the basis of prior period amounts adjusted for expected price level changes. Most major financial service institutions publish indices that can be used to adjust historical cost data. When using prior period expense levels to project expenses for future periods, it is necessary to adjust base period costs to neutralize the effects of large and/or unusual items. Similarly, it is necessary to adjust future period estimates for anticipated expenditures of a nonrecurring nature.

Although the use of economic indicators is a sound means of projecting expenses, it must be recognized that other variables can, and probably will, impact future expense levels. For instance, depreciation expenses and/or costs of capital determinations will be affected by anticipated acquisitions and disposals of fixed assets. Future floor space charges will be affected by lease escalation charges, lease renewal options, and planned expansion or relocation of facilities. When projecting administrative expenses, staffing levels cannot be ignored.

Increased or decreased staffing will necessarily impact expenses such as supplies, telephone, certain equipment rental expenses, and/or the cost of purchased clerical and professional services. Natural expense categories cannot be projected in a vacuum. Successful budgeting can be achieved only when all expense categories are viewed as a fully integrated system of related variables.

Capital Budgets

Capital budgets are prepared for anticipated acquisitions of major assets such as property, buildings, and equipment. The preparation of the capital expenditure budget is a relatively simple process. The budget itself is merely a listing of planned capital acquisitions and the corresponding cost of each item. Annual depreciation charges associated with capital acquisitions should be included within the operating expense budget for the appropriate accounting period. The important factor relating to capital budgets is not the documet itself or the amounts contained therein, but the rationale employed in determining what expenditures to include in the budget and what expenditures to defer and/or exclude all together. It is in this regard that managers and administrators must employ sound evaluation techniques in order to justify specific expenditures. Some factors to consider are:

- The necessity of the expenditure;
- The availability of external funding to cover the cost of the expenditure or a portion thereof;
- The cost savings and/or avoidance that will be realized as a result of the expenditure; and
- The relative cost of capital related to the acquisition.

A rational decision with respect to committing funds for the acquisition of major assets can be made only after considering the real need for the proposed purchase. The process should begin with the initiator of the request. Ideally, initiators should be responsible for developing a formal proposal or request for expenditure. The basis of a sound proposal is the statement of need. The statement of need should address the purpose of the proposed expenditure and the related justification in terms of cost savings or avoidance. It is a prudent practice to require initiators to identify alternatives to the proposed acquisition and to quantify the relative monetary impact of all alternatives. Some capital expenditures are unavoidable. Commitments made in grant proposals often require the acquisition of particular assets to accomplish the objectives set forth within the proposal. In these cases, need and cost/benefit relationships may be secondary considerations; nevertheless, they should be included within the evaluation and approval process. The availability of external funding does not relieve managers and administrators of their oversight responsibility for ensuring prudent management of funds.

When considering the acquisition of a capital asset, one should factor the opportunity loss attributable to the expenditure into the cost/benefit analysis. In its simplest form, opportunity loss is defined as foregone investment income on the amount to be invested in the asset. While opportunity losses are not considered expenses with respect to the organization's financial accounting system, their impact in terms of the organization's financial strength can be significant, particularly when other justification factors prove to be questionable. One method of computing opportunity loss is to use a basic compound interest model. For example, the opportunity loss on a $15,000 personal computer configuration expected to last five years is calculated in the following manner, assuming an 8 percent interest rate:

Year	Amount	Rate	Cumulative Value
1	$15,000	8%	$16,200
2	16,200	8%	17,496
3	17,496	8%	18,896
4	18,896	8%	20,408
5	20,408	8%	22,041

Cumulative Value	-	Purchase Price	=	Opportunity Loss
$22,041	-	$15,000	=	$7,041

In the preceding example the actual cost of the asset, when considering the impact of the opportunity loss, is $22,041. This is the cost that should be used when evaluating alternatives such as leasing the equipment. However, for budgeting purposes, the actual purchase price, $15,000, should be used because it reflects the actual amount of the anticipated cash outlay.

Capital expenditure budgets typically include amounts associated with the purchase of fixed assets as well as amounts associated with certain lease arrangements. For financial accounting purposes, the cost of a lease that results in the lessee obtaining title to the leased property at the end of the lease term with no additional considerations or at a price substantially below anticipated market value must be capitalized. The theory underlying this treatment is that, regardless of when title to the property is transferred, the substance of such a transaction implies that the organization has acquired an asset at the time the transaction is executed. These types of transactions are considered capital expenditures for budgeting purposes because of the relatively large financial commitment, the impact of the lease terms on the financial statements, and the end result of the transaction; that is, an asset will ultimately be acquired.

Capital expenditure budgets are not mutually exclusive with operating expense budgets. The acquisition of a capital asset through a direct purchase will result in periodic depreciation charges to the organization's operating expenses. Consequently, the depreciation expense associated with anticipated purchases should be included within the operating expense budget for the appropriate period. Similarly, amortization expenses associated with capital lease arrangements should be included with operating expenses for budgeting purposes.

The Budget Period

Operating budgets and capital expenditure forecasts are normally prepared for the next twelve-month accounting period. While the aggregate budget provides a planning and control mechanism in terms of an organization's short-term goals, a degree of refinement is necessary in order to use these tools effectively in the daily operation of the organization. It is highly recommended that annual budgets be detailed by month for use in measuring performance in a timely manner. Monthly review of budget variances enables managers and administrators to react aberrant situations before they become unmanageable problems.

Some organizations prepare long-term financial forecasts for five and sometimes even ten years. While long-term planning efforts of this nature contribute to the organization's overall strategy development process, they are of little use in terms of their financial reliability. Use of this type of long-term forecast should be limited to developing general plans and strategies. Each year, the long-term forecast should be refined to reflect current economic trends and developments.

The Flexible Budget

Flexible budgeting (changing forecasts on an interim basis to reflect unanticipated occurrences) is a common practice among tax-exempt organizations. This practice normally occurs when unanticipated revenues facilitate and/or necessitate changes in the level of an organization's operations. For instance, an unexpected bequeathal may prompt an organization's governing body to initiate a new community service program, one that was not previously budgeted for. Under the flexible budgeting approach, the organization would increase budgeted expenses to reflect the increased level of operations. Failure to adjust budgeted expenses will result in invalid performance measurement and could ultimately contribute to unrealistic forecasts for future periods. While flexible budgeting is necessary in some circumstances, caution should be exercised to prevent the arbitrary changing of budgets to accommodate management expectations. Budget maintenance should occur only when a reasonable rationale exists to justify the change.

Cash Flow versus Budgets

Although budgeting is related to the organization's relative financial strength in terms of its liquid assets (cash and short-term investments), an organization's budget in the short term may differ significantly from anticipated cash flows. It is not uncommon for an organization to budget capital expenditures and operating expenses at levels which exceed expected revenues. In these cases, the negative cash flow will necessitate using existing surplus to cover the shortfall. Although consistent budgeting in this manner will result in insolvency, occasional periods of negative cash flow are not necessarily harmful to an organization's financial security.

Operational Considerations—Planning and Budgeting

In tax-exempt organizations, financial planning, particularly in terms of budget preparation and prospective financial forecasting, is typically thought of as a pure financial function. While financial managers are ultimately responsible for producing the governing documents, the integrity of the data contained within these documents is dependent upon the mutual efforts of both financial and operational personnel. Financial managers are equipped with the necessary analytical capabilities. Managers of the organization's operations are knowledgeable about what resources are required to get the job done. Accordingly, financial and operational personnel must coordinate their respective activities as they relate to all aspects of prospective financial analysis.

RETROSPECTIVE FINANCIAL REVIEW

The financial data presented in financial statements, budgets, and other financial reports become the basis from which managers and administrators review performance and decide upon future courses of action. In this regard, there are several analytical tools available to assist managers annd administrators in reviewing financial data and evaluating past performance. Financial statements can be analyzed in terms of relative relationships between the component parts, or they can be analyzed in terms of their overall relationship with projected results. Operating expenses can be reviewed to identify significant variances from budget projections so that justifications from management can be sought and analyzed. Two commonly used tools are ratio analysis and pro forma reports.

Ratio Analysis

Ratio analysis is a tool whereby balance sheet line items are examined in terms of their relationship with one another or in terms of their relationship with revenues, expenses, or another independent variable. The following paragraphs discuss some of the more common ratios that exempt organizations can use to measure the effectiveness of past performance.

Current Ratio. The current ratio is a measure of an organization's liquidity. The ratio is calculated by dividing current assets by current liabilities. A high current ratio is desirable; it indicates that the organization is better able to withstand temporary periods of cash shortfalls. Examination of the current ratio at the end of an isolated accounting period may be misleading. It is better to examine trends over several months. Although a high ratio is desirable, a sharp, sustained increase in the current ratio may be an indication of problems with respect to the collectability of the organization's accounts receivable. The component parts of the numerator and the denominator should be examined as a means of explaining significant variations.

A more precise indicator of an organization's liquidity can be developed by using a variation of the current ratio. The variation involves adjusting the numerator to reflect cash and other current assets that can be easily converted to cash. Current assets that will not be converted to cash, such as prepaid expenses, are excluded from the numerator.

Operating Expense Ratio. An organization's ability to meet its current obligations can be measured by dividing the balance of its cash and cash equivalents at the end of an accounting period by its average monthly operating expense. An unfavorable trend from one accounting period to the next could be an indicator of aberrant situations with respect to expense levels and/or of cash flow problems attributable to the collectability of accounts receivable.

Liquidity Ratio. A general indication of an organization's financial strength can be computed by dividing total assets by total liabilities. Although there is a direct correlation between this ratio and the relative strength of the organization's surplus, a high ratio does not necessarily imply that the organization can meet its obligations in a timely manner. The level of fixed assets, if it is disproportionate to the total asset base, could distort the results. For this reason, it is suggested that the liquidity ratio be used solely to measure relative financial strength, and that the current ratio or a variation thereof be used to measure liquidity.

Revenue Ratio. Given the assumption that fixed assets are acquired and used in the revenue production process, the effectiveness with which the assets are used can be measured by dividing revenues for an accounting period by the average level of assets. Comparisons from one accounting period to the next are generally valid; however, the effects of significant acquisitions should be recognized when analyzing trends.

Employment Ratio. Revenues and their relative level of acceptability in terms of an organization's employment base can be measured by computing the dollar value of revenues per full-time employee. Decreases in this ratio from one accounting period to the next could be an indication of overstaffing or underutilization of the workforce.

Average Collection Period. Exempt organizations that are involved in the sale of products or services to the general public or to other business entities may wish to examine the average collection period for their accounts receivable. The average collection period, in days, is computed by multiplying the accounts receivable balance by 365 and dividing the result by annual credit sales. The result of this calculation indicates the number of days of sales that are uncollected at the end of the accounting period. Although the threshold of acceptability with respect to average collection periods will vary from organization to organization, a reasonable collection period to expect is approximately thirty to forty-five days.

Productivity Ratio. Productivity, in terms of an organization's "bottom line," can be measured by dividing net income (revenues less expenses) by revenues. This type of analysis provides managers and administrators with a clear insight into the organization's performance because it focuses on more than just revenue levels. Periods of increasing revenue that otherwise look favorable may be, in actuality, unfavorable if expenses increase at a more rapid rate.

Solvency. An organization's solvency can be measured by dividing its surplus by the total asset base. The resulting percentage gives an indication of overall financial strength. A high percentage is desirable because it indicates that there is a relatively small level of outside obligations which the organization needs to satisfy. The ratio for solvent organizations will always be positive; a negative ratio indicates insolvency because negative surplus necessarily means that liabilities are greater than assets.

Other Ratios. There are numerous ratios that can be developed to measure aspects of an organization's financial position or its overall performance. Due to the diversity among exempt organizations, there is no standard set of financial indicators that can be applied on a uniform basis. Managers and administrators should examine the unique attributes of their organization and develop a set of financial indicators to suit their particular circumstances.

Pro Forma Statements

The meaningfulness of an organization's financial statements can be enhanced when the statements are analyzed in conjunction with financial projections for the corresponding accounting period. Pro forma financial statements contain three data elements—actual statistics, projected statistics, and the variance between actual and projected data elements.

When preparing pro forma statements, it is beneficial to include as many line items as possible. Statements that show actual versus projected results by line of business or operational segment are preferable to summary statements. Business segment reporting enables statement users to isolate problems that could easily be overlooked in the summary statement format. When analyzing variances, the existence of an unfavorable variance may not always be an indication of poor performance. For example, unexpected revenues may be the reason for unfavorable expense variances. The incremental profit in situations such as these should be examined to evaluate the relative impact of the variance.

In order to be more meaningful, financial projections should be updated as often as circumstances warrant. Management decisions should not be based upon unrealized goals.

SUMMARY

Tax-exempt organizations are not unlike their taxable counterparts with respect to their need for accurate and timely financial information. The accuracy of financial information is directly related to the organization's system of internal controls. The existence of an adequate internal control system also provides the organization with a means to comply with applicable tax law and to enhance administrative efficiencies with respect to its daily operations.

Prospective financial analysis enables an organization to establish its short- and long-term goals and facilitates planning efforts in terms of staffing levels, fund-raising activities, and capital expenditure programs. Prospective financial analysis is the basis for planning the activities of an exempt organization.

Retrospective financial review is necessary to measure performance in terms of an organization's relative financial performance and strength. Examination of historical financial information enhances planning efforts.

Select Bibliography

Baker, Dale E. "Accounting for Restricted and Unrestricted Funds." *Journal of Accountancy* (May 1988): 68-76.

Fertig, Paul E., Donald F. Istvan, and Homer J. Mottice. *Using Accounting Information.* New York: Harcourt, Brace & World, 1965.

Hopkins, Bruce R. *The Law of Tax-Exempt Organizations.* 5th ed. New York: John Wiley and Sons, 1987.

Miller, Martin A., ed. *GAAP Guide.* San Diego: Harcourt Brace Jovanovich, 1988.

Phelan, Marilyn E. *Nonprofit Enterprises: Law and Taxation.* Wilmette, Illinois: Callaghan & Company, 1985.

Research Institute of America, Inc. *Federal Tax Coordinator.* 2d ed. Vol. D (Part 2). New York: 1990.

Sawyer, Lawrence B. *The Practice of Modern Internal Auditing.* Altamore Springs, Florida: The Institute of Internal Auditors, 2d ed. 1981.

Schattke, Rudolph W., Howard G. Jensen, and Virginia L. Bean. *Financial Accounting.* Boston: Allyn and Bacon, Inc., 1975.

Sughrue, Robert N. "Taxation Issues in a Nonprofit Environment." *Management Accounting* (August 1988): 57-60.

Treusch, Paul E. *Tax-Exempt Charitable Organizations.* 3d ed. 1988.

U.S. Department of the Treasury. Internal Revenue Service. *Tax-Exempt Status for Your Organization.* Publication 557.

U.S. Department of the Treasury. Internal Revenue Service. *Tax Information for Private Foundations and Foundation Managers.* Publication 578, Rev. 1989.

U.S. Department of the Treasury. Internal Revenue Service. *Tax on Unrelated Business Income of Exempt Organizations.* Publication 598, Rev. 1987.

U.S. Department of the Treasury. Internal Revenue Service. *Favorable Determination Letter.* Publication 794, Rev. 1986.

Van Voorhis, Robert H., Clarence L. Dunn, and Fritz A. McCameron. *Using Accounting in Business.* Belmont, California: Wadsworth Publishing Company, 1962.

Wacht, Richard F. *Financial Management in Nonprofit Organizations.* Atlanta: Georgia State University, 1984.

Index

About the Authors

ROBERT N. SUGHRUE is Manager of Fiscal Affairs for The Pittsburgh Research Institute in Pittsburgh, Pennsylvania.

MICHELLE L. KOPNSKI is an attorney with Springer, Bush, and Perry in Pittsburgh.